God Wants You to Do His Will

The Meat of the Word
for Christians Today
Volume 1

God Wants You to Do His Will

by
Pastor Willie F. Pride, Jr.

Everlasting Publishing
Yakima, Washington

God Wants You to Do His Will

The Meat of the Word for Christians Today
Volume 1

by
Pastor Willie F. Pride, Jr.

All Bible verses are from
The King James Version

ISBN: 0-9778083-5-1
ISBN-13: 978-0-9778083-5-9

First Edition
Everlasting Publishing
P.O. Box 1061
Yakima, WA 98907-1061

*Truly, we thank God for His Word,
for heaven and earth will pass away,
but God's Word will stand forever.*

I would like to dedicate this book to my late father, the Rev. Willie F. Pride, Sr., who introduced me at a young age to Jesus, the One who is the Subject of this book; and to my mother, Florence, who still studies the Word of God with me, as we delight in it together.

Pastor Willie F. Pride, Jr.

Table of Contents

The Man on Easy Street
Luke 16:14-31

Turn with me in your Bibles, to the 16th chapter of St. Luke this morning, where our sermon scripture is coming from today.

Somebody would say this morning, "Is there a Word from the Lord?" I want to say, there's always a Word from God. Amen. It may not come in the way you think it should come. It may not come as a lightning bolt, but sometimes it comes as a still, quiet voice that says, "I'm God."

We truly thank God for you today, for the Bible tells us that faith cometh by hearing. We have that still, quiet voice that says to you and to me that everything will be all right. It says to neither turn right nor turn left; but there's always a Word from God. The 16th chapter of St. Luke, beginning of the 14th verse, reads to us this morning:

14. And the Pharisees also, who were covetous, heard all these things: and they derided him.
15. And he said unto them, Ye are they which justify yourselves before men; but God knoweth your hearts: for that which is highly esteemed among men is abomination in the sight of God.
16. The law and the prophets were until John: since that time the kingdom of God is preached, and every man presseth into it.
17. And it is easier for heaven and earth to pass, than one tittle of the law to fail.
18. Whosoever putteth away his wife, and marrieth another, committeth adultery: and whosoever marrieth her that is put away from her husband committeth adultery.
19. There was a certain rich man, which was clothed in purple and fine linen, and fared sumptuously every day:
20. And there was a certain beggar named Lazarus, which was laid at his gate, full of sores,
21. And desiring to be fed with the crumbs which fell from the rich man's table: moreover the dogs came and licked his sores.

22. And it came to pass, that the beggar died, and was carried by the angels into Abraham's bosom: the rich man also died, and was buried;

23. And in hell he lift up his eyes, being in torments, and seeth Abraham afar off, and Lazarus in his bosom.

24. And he cried and said, Father Abraham, have mercy on me, and send Lazarus, that he may dip the tip of his finger in water, and cool my tongue; for I am tormented in this flame.

25. But Abraham said, Son, remember that thou in thy lifetime receivedst thy good things, and likewise Lazarus evil things: but now he is comforted, and thou art tormented.

(Oh, bless His name today. I want to go on from there, but I need to read a little bit more.)

26. And beside all this, between us and you there is a great gulf fixed: so that they which would pass from hence to you cannot; neither can they pass to us, that would come from thence.

27. Then he said, I pray thee therefore, father, that thou wouldest send him to my father's house:

28. For I have five brethren; that he may testify unto them, lest they also come into this place of torment.

29. Abraham saith unto him, They have Moses and the prophets; let them hear them.

30. And he said, Nay, father Abraham: but if one went unto them from the dead, they will repent.

31. And he said unto him, If they hear not Moses and the prophets, neither will they be persuaded, though one rose from the dead.

Let us pray.

Our Father and our God, we thank You now for what You've done. We thank You for the Word today, Lord God. We ask You, heavenly Father, if You would open up my mouth. We ask You, heavenly Father, that You would use me in a mighty way. Not my will, but Thy will be done.

Oh, heavenly Father, as we celebrate this get-up morning, this resurrection day, Lord God, we praise You for what You've done. You were victorious. You held the keys of death in Your hand, and

You got up with all power. Thank You, Lord God, that we, too, one day will rise up and meet You in the clouds and go home to be with You. Thank You, Lord God, for what You've done, and are doing, and are going to do in the service this day. In Jesus' name we pray, thank God, thank God, thank God.

We see from this passage of Scripture this morning, in Luke 16:19, that there was a certain man which was clothed in purple and fine linen, and the Scripture said that he fared well. He was a rich man. He had a lot of things going for him.

I want to talk about this morning, the thought of the subject that you might carry home with you this morning: "The Man on Easy Street." You might say, "But Pastor, that's not a message for Easter Sunday." That's not a message that people really want to hear. They want to hear something about Jesus jumping up out of the grave; but I want to go a little different way with you this morning.

There were two men, as you heard in the passage. One was a rich man and one was a man by the name of the Lazarus, as we read in the story. It says that this rich man had everything. He had the whole world, as we say, by the tail, and he had everything going his way—everything. Do you not know, regardless of how much you have or how much that you ever possess, you're going to leave here one day, and all those things that you have or tried to develop and put together, they're going to stay right here?

The word grows out of the expression of the English language, denoting wealth, which means that he was a rich man, one who has much of the world's goods, with no worry about financial matters or any material things. This is the rich man now. In the language of today, this man was a man on Easy Street, for this man had it made. The text turns the light on one who had everything he could wish for, and can rightly be called the man on Easy Street. Jesus did not refer to him as such, but when he finished describing him and telling what he had, where he lived, and how he had behaved and reacted to other people, he was a man on Easy Street. Briefly, if you will, this morning, let's glance back to the text and get a glimpse of him as Jesus turns the flashlight of time on this notorious character, in order to make up our minds as to what and who he was. This was a certain rich man, which was clothed in purple and fine linen, and not only that, it says that he dined exclusively every day.

While at the window of time, Jesus raised a certain question, so we could look upon another man in the same town, but in a different situation. They had many things in common that brought them together. Number one, they were of the human race. Number two, they were members of the Jewish family. Number three, they were both men with burning passions and capacity for greatness. They both were social beings with the desire for goodwill, to and from their fellow man. Both had the same type of belief in God.

Do you not know, sisters and brothers, it's more than being religious? It's more than just believing in God, for Jesus said that He is the Way, and no man comes to the Father, but by Him. Oh, bless His name today. So we see that this man who had everything going for him, he was the same as Lazarus except for one certain condition existed that they did not have in common, which kept them apart. One was rich, and one was poor.

You might say this morning, "Oh, but Pastor, I should have what Trump has, or what the Gettys have, or what some others have." But let me tell you today, whatever you might have, nothing should be before God, for He is a jealous God. He doesn't want mother or father or sister or brother, or anything else to be put above Him.

Jesus turned the light on the certain rich man. He also turned it on a certain poor man, for you could hardly know one without knowing the other. However, in describing the man on Easy Street, Jesus pointed out his qualities, not his name, not his possessions. In describing the man at the gate, He points out that the beggar, Lazarus, lay at the gate, full of sores, and he wanted the crumbs from the rich man's table.

We also see in these two verses that Jesus wrote the biography of the two most noted men in the New Testament. He says that one did nothing but grabbed the scraps. The other was the one that fared like many people do today. The one man in this picture was the victim of circumstances. He had ill health, and he had marred progress, to where he was living real bad. He lived off charity and the gifts of the people in the community. He was in such bad shape that the people called him the sore man, or Lazarus.

A man's condition usually governs his desires. Lazarus was a sick man. He wasn't able to work; therefore, he would be satisfied with the dogs' portion, the crumbs that fell from the rich man's table. But rather than let him have the crumbs, the rich man turned the dogs loose. I want to tell you this morning, many of us are living high on the hog, as they say, but all of our money and all of our good works won't get us into the kingdom of God.

I look this morning at Jesus, who died on the cross. He died on the cross for your sins and my sins, and for the sins of the world. You might say this morning, is there a place for those that are contrary to God? Oh, yes there is, and I want to tell you, there is a place for those who have been washed in the blood of the Lamb.

I don't know about you this morning; maybe you don't have relationship with Jesus. I want to tell you today, nobody can do you like the Lord. Nobody can do you like Jesus. I don't care what you might have, nobody can give you joy like Jesus can give. Nobody can give you peace like Jesus can give. Nobody can heal your body like Jesus can. I'm mindful this morning, He gives a joy that the world didn't give and the world can't take away.

As we move on here this morning, the dogs proved to be more humane than their master. Instead of snarling and tearing Lazarus apart, the story says the dogs licked his sores. I remember when I was a boy growing up in Tennessee, there were times that we had sores, and if you had a dog, that dog would come and lick the sore that you had; and in a short time that sore would get well.

God can do all things but fail. There's something about the Lord. He's got more healing in the hem of His garment than any drugstore in the land. He can move like nobody else can move. Whatever burdens you have, you can take your burdens to the Lord, and you can leave them there. I'm glad this morning that Jesus is still saving. He's still sanctifying. He's still giving sight to the blind. He's still raising up. He's still baptizing, and He's still filling.

I don't care what the world might say: my God is in control. Let nobody tell you this morning that the Lord doesn't know what's going on, for He sits high and He looks low. Nobody, today, can do you like Jesus. Nobody, today, can do you like the Lord. I feel, this morning, that the Lord is calling, and let me tell you today, He's not calling black or white, red, yellow, or any other color, but He's calling the people that have been washed in the blood of the Lamb.

The Lord Jesus will turn your midnight into day. He will turn you around. He will, this morning, direct your path. You can stand on His Word. I'm glad today. I'm glad the Lord is in control. Put your hand, not in my hand, but put your hand in God's hand, and He will direct your path. He will turn your midnights into day! He will! Oh, bless His name today.

As I move on here today, the Scripture says the dogs proved to be more humane than their master because instead of tearing Lazarus apart, they licked his sores. God sometimes can get the hearts of dogs before He can get the hearts of men. "What are you saying today, Pastor?" I'm glad this morning, for the young people that are here, for Jesus said, unless you come as a little child, you cannot enter the kingdom of God. "What are you talking about, Pastor?" I'm saying, you need to have a childlike attitude. You need to have an attitude of forgiveness and forgetfulness. You need to have an attitude of knowing that though you hurt me, I'm going to love you anyhow.

Do you ever see kids, they can be fighting with one another one minute and in the next few minutes they're playing and loving one another? We adults ought to learn something from that. As Jesus said, unless you come as a little child, you can't enter the kingdom of God.

I'm glad this morning. I'm glad today for the mighty Lamb of God. I'm glad for the Word, for there's power in the Word, the Word of God. You can stand today, regardless of what men may say. You can stand on the Word of God. I tell young people and old people everywhere I go, "Heaven and earth are going to pass away, but the Word of God is going to stand forever." I tell you today, whatever you want to be, it's not in you, but it's in the Word. You can stand on the Word of God. I'm thankful to the Lord today. Oh, bless His name! Oh, bless His name.

As we see this morning, only God knew He was lowering the curtain on the closing scenes of time for both men. Neither one knew what was going to happen, and let me tell you this morning, you don't know what's going to happen. You might say to me, "Pastor, I've got my future in my own hands." You've got to put your future in God's hand. You've got to put your life in God's hand, for He's the only One who can turn midnight into day. He's the only One. Oh, bless His name.

I'm mindful of the story of a man who was waiting on the Lord, and the story goes that this man got his house in order, everything spick-and-span. Everything was looking good. This man had everything ready and he was waiting for the Lord's coming. The Lord had told him He would come and see about him.

But let me tell you this morning, you don't have to wait on the Lord. He's already here! You don't have to look for Him. He's already here! My Bible tells me, if you draw nigh unto Him, then He'll draw nigh unto you. He's already here!

This man was waiting on the Lord and he heard a knock at his door. He opened the door, and there was a man at the door. This man was unshaven, and this man needed a bath.

He said, "Sir, I saw your light on, and I thought I'd stop by. I want to know if you'll help me. I'm down and out, and I don't know where to go." This man that owned the house said, "Well, I don't know if I can help you or not," but God began to deal with his conscience at that same second, and the man opened the door. He said, "Come on in and clean yourself up. Don't mess anything up. When you get done, go out the side door. I've got a visitor coming." The man went in, and he got himself cleaned up, and he went about his business.

At about 11:30 there was another knock on the door. The man said, "I know this is the Lord, because God always comes between 11:30 and 12:00." (Thank God, we don't know when He will come.) The man opened the door, and there, standing at the door, was a lady with three small kids, and the lady was crying. She said, "Sir, my kids are hungry. We have been walking all day. We saw your light on, and we decided we would try and ask if you would help us." The man said, "There's nothing I can do for you." The man on Easy Street is saying, "There's nothing I can do for you."

Let me tell you, when God moves in your life, He'll turn you around. Oh, bless His name today! I see the kids have gotten a little quiet. Makes me want to go a little higher, but I'm glad today!

The man says, "Nothing I can do for you...but come on in, and clean up the kids. Get you something to eat, and don't mess anything up. When you get done, you go out the back door, and you go on about your business."

And then, about midnight, there was another knock on the door. The man said, "I know this is the Lord coming to see about me." And the story goes, when the man opened the door, there was a little child there. She was crying, tears running down her face. As she stood there crying, she said to the man, "I'm lost, and I was hoping you could help me find my way home." Then the man said, "I can't help you. I can't leave the house, because if I leave, the One that I'm looking for will come and I won't be here."

But let me tell you today, the conscience of a man is different than anything else. I might not be able to look in your window and see what you're doing, but God looks in. Hallelujah! He looks in your window, and He looks in your heart. I'm glad this morning!

And the man said to the girl, "Let me tell you, I won't just walk you part of the way, but I'll walk you all the way back." So he walked the little girl all the way home, and he got back to his house. He waited. At 12:30 a.m., nobody showed up. At 12:45 a.m., nobody showed up. 1:00 a.m., nobody showed up. The man went back into his room. He got down on his knees.

He said, "Lord, I don't understand this. You promised that You were going to come and see about me. You promised me that You were going to come by my house. You promised me." (Oh, bless God.) "You promised me." (Oh, bless His name.) "But You promised me, Jesus, You were going to see about me."

And all of a sudden, a Voice came to the man, and the Voice said, "I came. I came as an old man, who you gave a shave to. I came as a woman and three small kids. I came as a little girl that you didn't take part of the way, but you took all the way home. I came today."

Let me tell you this morning, many of us are looking for Jesus to come in a different way. But He comes — oh, bless God — He comes as He will. I'm glad this morning. If you're waiting on the Lord, He's already here. You don't have to look for Him. Oh, bless His name! He's already been found.

I'm glad this morning, for what the Lord is doing. You can stand on the Word of God. Let me tell you this morning, as I come to a close, look at Jesus, the mighty Lamb of God, blood running down from His hands and His feet. He didn't say a mumbling word, but, "Father." He was hanging there on the cross for your sins and for my sins and for the sins of the world, but He didn't say a mumbling word. I'm glad.

I'm glad for the young people today. They may not understand all that I'm saying, but let me tell you today, the Word says, "faith cometh by hearing, and hearing by the Word of God. And how can you hear without the preacher? And how can they preach unless they be sent?"

Oh, look at Jesus. He died on the cross for your sins and my sins, blood running down from His hands and His feet. We saw in the Sunday School lesson this morning that Thomas said, "Unless I can put my hand in His hand, unless I can put my hand in His side, I won't believe He's alive, or risen from the dead."

Jesus said, "Blessed are they that haven't seen, but believe by faith." Do you have the faith today, to know that Jesus is alive? He's alive this morning — oh, bless His name — with all power in His hand! I'm glad! I'm glad that He died for the sins of the world. I'm glad that they put Him in that cold, dark tomb. I'm glad He stayed there all day Saturday — oh, bless God! I feel something now — and all night Saturday night. I'm glad! I'm glad! I'm glad He lay there. Oh, glory to God!

He bruised the serpent's head when He lay down, and one day we're going to lay down. One day we're going to die and go to be with Him. But I'm glad that on that Sunday morning, they rolled the stone away. It was a big stone. No one man could push that stone away. But they rolled the stone away, the angels did, the messengers of God. I'm glad they rolled it back. The Word says, when they rolled the stone away, my Savior began to get up. He began to shed His grave clothes. And when He shed His grave clothes, He got up out of that tomb. When He got up out of that tomb, He got up with all power in His hand.

I don't know about you this morning, but you ought to be able to get up and tell somebody, "I know the Lord. He's been good to me."

You ought to be able to get up and tell somebody, "Jesus has turned my midnights into day."

You ought to be able to get up and tell somebody, "I know the Lord will be a doctor for me."

You ought to be able to get up and tell somebody, "I know the Lord will be a way-maker."

You ought to be able to get up and tell somebody, "Nobody can do me like the Lord."

You ought to be able to get up and tell the dying world, "I know the Lord. He has been so good to me. He has been a mother to me. He has been a lawyer for me."

I have to reminisce for just a little while. My dad died just about a month ago, and every now and then, I find myself thinking back on him. Oh, bless His name, glory to God. I find myself thinking about my dad and the other day I was fooling around with a key ring, and that's the key ring that belonged to my dad. As I was fooling around, and I'd never done that before, I took the little ring, and I put on my finger. I thought about it. I thought, my dad used to wear this ring. It was his Mason ring.

But let me tell you this morning, it's not so much that I'll not see him again, but Jesus said, "so a man live, will live again." And I want to tell you today, we're going to live again on the other side. Let nobody tell you that there's no hope, because there's all hope in Jesus. I'm glad this morning!

I don't know about you, but if Jesus hadn't gotten up from the grave with all power, I believe, today, I'd probably be fishing somewhere or doing something else. But He got up with all power! All power was in His hand!

If you're here this morning, maybe you're out of a church home. Maybe you've never accepted the Lord as your personal Savior. Maybe you've never repented of your sins. Somebody would say this morning, "I came to Jesus as I was. I was wounded and I was naked and I was hungry, when I found in Him a resting place. And He has made me glad." Oh, glory to God! If you're here this morning, and you've never accepted the Lord as your Savior, you can accept Him right now.

Let me go a little further today. I can't think of a better day to come to the Lord than today. If you're here today and you have not accepted Jesus as your personal Savior, you need to come now. Let me tell you this morning, you can't clean yourself up. Nobody can clean you up but Jesus. If you're here this morning, and you've never repented of your sins, you can come now and ask the Lord to come into your life, to come into your heart. If you're here this morning, you can come now, just as you are.

You can accept Jesus right now, if you pray this prayer with me:

"Father God, I know that I am a sinner and my sins have separated me from you. Father, please forgive me right now. I want to turn away from my sinful life and turn toward you. I believe that your Son, Jesus Christ, died on the cross for my sins, and on the third day, You raised Him from the dead, and now He is at Your right hand. I invite Jesus to come into my heart and become the Lord of my life from this day forward. Please send your Holy Spirit to help me obey You, and to do Your will for the rest of my life. In Jesus' name I pray, Amen."

True Worshipers
John 4:22-26

We really thank God today for what He has done. We thank the Lord this morning for your testimonies. Would you turn with me in your Bibles to the book of St. John, the fourth chapter?

You may ask the question today, "Is there a Word from the Lord?" I want to say, there is a Word from the Lord, in the fourth chapter of St. John. I want to say, before we get into the message, that the reason the church is like it is today, is because the ones in the church are not rooted and grounded in Jesus Christ. You might be thinking, "What are you saying, Pastor? Why would you make a statement like that?" Well, I have evidence to back it up. First of all, because we can see within the church, there are many that are falling away. There are many, this morning, who it started out with the Lord Jesus Christ, and we see them one month, six months, six years, 20 years, and 30 years from that day, and they have fallen away from the Lord.

I've come to the conclusion today that you must know for yourself that Christ is the center of your life, in every situation, because if He is not, the devil will always present something to bring you down, because someone did not say or do what you felt they should have said or done. We see that, time and time again, but the Bible must be fulfilled. As we read our Bibles this morning, nothing should surprise you, in terms of what's happening, not only in the world, but what's happening in the church, for the Bible says that God will start at the household of faith. God's purging and cleansing process will start in this place. It's already in the world. The devil already has the ones in the world. It will start at the household of God. I'm grateful to God that I can see evidence of that right now, this morning. (We will get into the message.) Last Sunday, this building was practically full. We had 18 kids just in the Sunday School class, not including all the other activities that were part of last Sunday. After the message last Sunday, we had two people come up as candidates for baptism. They accepted the Lord and said they wanted to be baptized. We're grateful to God this morning that in the midst of all that's going on, God truly know and cares. I've come to the conclusion that only what we do for Christ will last; not what you do for the pastor, not what you do for the church, but what you do for Him. It is the only thing that will last. Heaven and earth will pass away, but the Word of God will stand forever.

In the book of St. John, the fourth chapter beginning at the 22nd verse, it says to us:

22. Ye worship ye know not what: we know what we worship: for salvation is of the Jews.
23. But the hour cometh, and now is, when the true worshipers shall worship the Father in spirit and in truth: for the Father seeketh such to worship him.
24. God is a spirit: and they that worship him must worship him in spirit and in truth.
25. The woman said unto him, I know that Messias cometh, which is called Christ; when he is come, he will tell us all things.
26. Jesus saith unto her, I speak that unto thee am he.

May God bless the reader and hearer of His holy Word. Let us pray at this time.

Our Father, we come to You this morning, and Lord God, as we come today, we come lifting up Your holy name. Oh, heavenly Father, we pray now for these that are here, for You said, "Faith comes by hearing and hearing by the Word of God, and how can they hear without the preacher, and how can they preach unless they be sent?"

Father, we pray for every minister that's lifting up your name. We pray, Lord God, for every believer that's standing up for the bloodstained banner of Jesus Christ. Lord God, we pray for the ones who have come to Everlasting this morning. We pray for the ones who had to leave. We pray, Lord God, for the ones who have a desire to be here and are not today.

Oh, heavenly Father, we pray now that You will use these lips of clay: not my will, but Thy will be done. We pray, Lord God, that You will use me in a mighty way. We pray for our families that we're leaving behind. Oh, heavenly Father, we thank You, right now. Touch, Lord God, every part of our service, every meeting that takes place in this building. We pray, Lord God, that You will get the glory, in Jesus' name. Now Lord, bless us in a mighty way. In Jesus' name we pray, and we give You glory right now, in Jesus' name. Thank God, thank God, thank God.

Our subject this morning, that we want to talk about today, is "True Worshipers." Would you say it with me? "True worshipers." This week I had a woman come to me. As we were talking, she said to me, "Well, Pastor," she said, "I will not accept Christ, because there are too many non-caring hypocrites in the church." Let me say that again. She said, "I will not accept Christ, because there are too many non-caring hypocrites in the church." I said to her, "Sister, why would you let the devil get you caught up into what others are doing?" I said, "Can't you see that's a trick of the enemy? Can't you see, that's what the devil would have you to believe, and think you shouldn't come, because of what others are doing or not doing?" And I said to her, as I carried on this conversation with her, "Don't worry about what others are doing. You get your mind on the Lord. You get your heart fixed and yourself together, and everything else will fall in place." I said to her, "Don't you worry about what others are doing. You just try to get yourself right with God, and if you get yourself right with God, God will truly bless you."

But she was very argumentative, and she went on to talk about this one and that one, and she said, "I'll mention names." I said, "That's not necessary, Sister, because if you're looking for a perfect church, you'll never find it, for every church has its devils. Every church has its gossipers. Every church has its no-gooders, and on down the line." I said to her, "Even with Jesus, Jesus had twelve, and one of those twelve was a devil." I said, "You don't try to figure it out. You just follow Jesus, and He will do the work in your life."

This is what I want to talk about this morning, "True Worshipers." It says in the 23rd verse:

"But the hour cometh, and now is, when the true worshipers shall worship the Father in spirit and in truth: for the Father seeketh such to worship him."

Do you know, this morning, Jesus is looking for true worshipers? He's looking for those who will worship Him in spirit and in truth. That we should seek God seems most natural and proper. Poor, ignorant, sinful and helpless creatures that we are, we should be insensible and infuriated if we did not seek Him. Who alone can supply our needs? Only Jesus can supply our needs today. Only Jesus can pardon our errors. Only Jesus can secure our happiness. But that God should seek us seems strange.

The Bible says, as we read, that true worshipers must worship Him in spirit and in truth. We have here an instance of truth, that

God says our ways are not His ways. You might say, "Pastor, my ways are God's ways. My thoughts are His thoughts." Oh, no, they're not. But we are to be so close to God that we know that everywhere we go, we carry God with us. Everything we do, we are to recognize that it's God who has control of every situation.

I had some things happen to me this month and I had to make some decisions. Do you know that I could not rely upon my own decisions? I had to rely on God. I had to turn those things over to Him, asking Him to work them out. My wife asked me a couple days ago, "What do you think about this?" I told her I didn't know. Well, let me tell you this morning, you ought to come to a point in your life that you don't know, but when you pray and seek the Lord, you ought to know that for true worshipers, when they worship God, all things work together; for my Bible tells me in Romans 8:28, "And we know that all things work together for good to them that love God, to them who are the called according to his purpose." Not just some things, but *all things* work to your good, if you love God. I'm glad that all things are working to the good of true worshipers today. All things are working to the good of those that love Him today, and I love Him this morning.

I'm mindful of one of the small kids, as they gave a review from the Sunday school this morning, a little boy didn't say very much, but one thing he said before he took his seat was, "I love Jesus." True worshipers ought to love God with their hearts, their souls and their minds. True worshipers ought to lift up the name of Jesus. I'm glad this morning, everywhere I go, I can lift up the name of Jesus. Let me tell you this morning, when you start lifting Him up, you don't become popular, but Jesus said, if He be lifted up, He would draw all men.

I'm glad, I can preach the Word of God everywhere I go. Somebody will say that you need a church full to preach the Word of God, but let me tell you, the Bible says, "where two or three are gathered together in His name, He will be in the midst." Oh, I am glad this morning, I can lift up the name of Jesus. Let me tell you today, true worshipers don't need a church to lift up the name of Jesus. True worshipers don't need all of this pumped up stuff to worship the Lord. Everywhere you go, you ought to be able to worship the Lord.

I have a joy this morning that the world didn't give me and the world can't take away. I'm glad today, knowing and believing that true worship means abiding one with another. Somebody will say this morning, "I can worship God in my home. I can worship God watching TV. I can worship God walking down the street." I would say this morning, "Yes," to all of that. But let me tell you today, it's something about the saints of God, when they abide together, where the Spirit of God is, that brings joy. It's something about fellowshipping with the saints of God. True worship brings about a change in a person's attitude. Let nobody tell you, "You don't have to come and lift up the name of Jesus." Jesus said that He would be in the midst of the ones who have come together in His name. Let me move on here this morning.

What God seeks is true worship of His people, His children. That the Father desires. For He says He seeks a sinner who worships not of the lips merely, but of the heart. Let me tell you this morning, there are many people today who say they love you from their mouth, but their heart is full of so many devilish things. Let me tell you this morning, you ought to have that love today, that not only comes from the lips, but comes from the heart. It ought to come from the mind. It ought to come from the inside. Jesus said, "If you have My love abiding in you, I will pour out of your belly rivers of living water."

Oh, I'm glad this morning that I'm a true worshiper of the Lord. I'm glad this morning that it's not a tradition, but I can worship the Lord in spirit and in truth. Let me tell you this morning, nobody ought to steal your joy. Everywhere you go, you ought to let your light shine. I see so many Christians around who have no joy. But Jesus said, "I came to give you life. I came to give you joy. I came to give you peace. I came to give you hope."

I'm glad this morning, that Jesus said, to worship Him, you must rejoice in faithfulness. Jesus said, "If you be faithful over a few things, I'll make you a ruler over many." As you look around today, you might say you don't see too many here, but you ought to remember that in true worship, Jesus wants us to get tangled up, tied up, and wrapped up in Him. Everywhere you go, somebody ought to know that you've been born again. Everywhere you go, somebody ought to know that you're in constant worship. Let me tell you this morning, you don't have to open your mouth to worship the Lord. You don't have to wave your hand to worship the Lord. You don't have to carry a Bible to worship the Lord. David said, "Thy Word have I hid in my heart, that I might not sin against thee."

I've got the Word of God down on the inside. Oh, bless His name today. True worshipers ought to worship the Lord in spirit and in truth. God seeks a true worshiper by manifesting himself. How can He manifest Himself in me? He gives me joy. Oh, bless His name. He gives me peace. Thank You, Lord, for the joy that I have that the world didn't give and the world can't take away. Thank You, Lord. Oh, bless His name. Everywhere I go, I'm going to let my light shine. I don't know about you this morning: I love the Lord. I'm mindful of the three wise men. The Bible says, when they went to look for the baby Jesus, they went with worship on their minds. You ought to go to the Lord lifting Him up. You ought to go to the Lord knowing, "I'm worshiping the Lord, not because of what Mama did or because of what the church is doing, but because I love the Lord." I worship the Lord everywhere I go. I worship the Lord in my automobile. I worship the Lord in my own home.

Let me tell you today, when the saints of God begin to worship the Lord, something happens on the inside. I have a strenuous job. On my job, so much is going on all the time. But sometimes I steal away. I go back in the office. Nobody is there, and I get on my knees, and I pray and ask the Lord to give me strength.

True worship. Everywhere you go, you ought to tell somebody, "I know the Lord has brought me a mighty long way. I know the Lord has been good to me." Somebody told me the other day, "If you didn't have the Lord, you wouldn't be able to do the job you do." I told them, "You're right about that." I've got the Lord, wrapped up, tied up, all on the inside of me, and everywhere I go, I lift Him up. Oh, bless His name today!

I don't know about how discouraged you might get sometimes, but you have to be able to go to the Fountain, the Fountain of life, and tell the Lord, "I need to be filled. I need to be filled up." I feel something now, moving on the inside of me. I don't need ten thousand people to say a word for the Lord, but everywhere I go, I can lift Him up. I can tell somebody, "Nobody can do you like the Lord." Oh, glory to God! Glory to God!

I talked to my sister-in-law this morning. When I talked with her, she was crying on the phone, but I told her, "God will take care of you. God will meet your every need. All you've got to do is get on your knees. Steal away from the family. Steal away from your husband. Steal away from your kids. Steal away from everybody. Get on your knees and talk with the Lord. Tell the Lord, 'I need You.' Tell the Lord, 'I need your help.' Tell the Lord, 'I need you right now,' and He will come in."

Let me move on here this morning. True worship ought to be in manifesting Him, by the power of God. What power could I have, that when the world is treating me badly, I can turn the other cheek? What power could I, a true worshiper have, when they lie about me? What power could I have, when everything might be against me? What power could I have, when my body is filled with pain? What power could I have, when nobody is my friend?

Let me tell you about that power today. It's not in the Baptist Church. That power is not something that man can give. That power is in Jesus Christ. And how can you get it this morning? Go down on your knees and talk with the Lord. I told my sister-in-law this morning, she doesn't need to look around. She can go down on her knees and begin to talk with the Lord, and He will make a way out of no way.

As I move on here today, why seek God? It is sometimes objected to Christian worship, that it assumes a Being delighting in His own praises, and so partaking of the infirmity of the human vanity, it is said that even the wise man isn't above this weakness. It is dishonoring to the Eternal to ascribe to Him any desire to delight Himself in honoration of the creatures who praise Him. But let me tell you this morning, you ought to have a praise for God. You ought to have a joy that the world didn't give and the world can't take away.

I'm glad this morning. I got up this morning and I can worship the Lord. I can lift Him up. I can praise His holy name. I don't need a church full of people to lift Him up. I can just go to my prayer closet and lift up the name of Jesus.

I want to share a testimony this morning. Let me call somebody, a lady by the name of Sister Minnie. Just a few years ago, she was on her deathbed. She had been saved for about 40 years, and Sister Minnie died last year in the nursing home. Let me give you her testimony today.

I would go visit her in the nursing home through the months and years. She had a bone disease and it was carrying her down, it seemed like, every month. I would see Sister Minnie, at one time she was weighing 160 pounds, then she was down to about 90. Let me tell you this morning, Sister Minnie had a testimony. Every time I would go into her room, she never had a frown on her face. Every time I would go in, she would tell me, "I love Jesus." She would say to me, "Reverend Pride, if you never see me again, I'm going to be with Jesus." Every time a nurse would come into her room, she would witness about what the Lord had done in her life. That's true worship in every sense. She died last year. But let me tell you today, she is somewhere around the throne of God, and she's worshiping the name of Jesus.

Let me call here today, Dr. Ralph Abernathy, who died just a few days ago, and I knew the man. I knew him well, and I want to close today with his testimony. Dr. Abernathy said to me just about a year ago, as he was coming to the airport, as a matter of fact, I brought him to the airport so he could get his plane back home, he said, "Pride, I want to tell you a story."

One thing about him, he was good at giving analogies, and he told me a story about a man that was a truck driver. This man was driving down the road one day, and as he was driving, something happened to the truck. The truck skidded off this embankment and tumbled down this big, old cliff. It turned and turned all the way to the bottom. Dr. Abernathy said when the truck stopped, the driver got out, he climbed out of the truck. He got on top of the truck and was sitting there. Dr. Abernathy said the driver looked up to some people who saw the truck go over the embankment. They came to the top and yelled down, "Brother, do want us to go get some help? Do you want us to find somebody, or send some help, send somebody down for you?"

Brother Abernathy said the truck driver looked up, and told them, "Keep on going in the direction you're going. Don't worry about me. Everything is under control. Don't worry about me. I've got the situation under control. I've gotten in touch with my boss man, and help is on the way."

Then Brother Abernathy said to me, "Pride, let me tell you something," and this was just last year, in September. He said, "You might hear about me dying one day. You might hear about me being killed one day. You might hear about me leaving this earth. Well, don't you worry about me. I've gotten in touch with my Savior. I'm in touch with Him. You just keep on preaching, keep on carrying on, keep on lifting up the name of Jesus."

When I read in the newspaper that he died, and the clipping is on the bulletin board, I said, "Thank you, Brother Abernathy. You told me that one day I was going to hear about you going on home to be with Jesus, but not to worry, and I should go on in the Lord's name. I'm going on today, in the Lord's name."

I want to challenge you this morning, regardless of what others might say or do, you go on in the Lord's name, and He will make a way for you. He will turn your midnights into day. He will, today. I know I'm right about it.

So I want to tell you today, true worship is calling on the name of the Lord. It's calling on Jesus while He's near. You can call on Him this morning, any morning, noon and night. It doesn't make any difference. You can call on the Lord, and He'll hear your prayer. Thank You, Jesus for what You're doing.

I can see Jesus this morning, hanging there on the cross, blood running down from His hands and His feet. (I am in revival now!) Look at the blood, oh, bless His name today, they hanged Him there. He was hanging there. They stretched Him wide. They pierced Him in the side. They nailed the nails in His hands. But He didn't say a mumbling word, but "Father, oh, Father, forgive them for they know not what they do." Forgive them today.

Can you tell somebody, "You may have lied about me, but I forgive you." "You may have slandered my name, but I forgive you." "You might have told dirty things about me, but I forgive you." "Maybe I haven't been the kind of Christian I should've been, but, God, forgive me today." I know He'll forgive you this morning. I can feel my help now. You're forgiven right now, if you put your hand in God's hands.

They took Jesus off that cross. Oh, glory! They took Him off that cross. They placed Him in that borrowed tomb. All day Saturday, all night Saturday night, He laid there. Oh, bless His name today. He laid there for you and for me. I want to tell you today, my God is not dead. Oh, He's not dead. He woke me up this morning. He started me on my way. Oh, glory, I feel it now. Oh, I feel it now!

Maybe you don't understand why I feel like this. I've got something moving on the inside of me. I've got something all in my feet. It's all in my hands.

Oh, Lord, I bless You today for what You are doing! Thank You, Lord, for opening doors that no man can shut! Thank You, Lord, oh, glory, thank You, Lord!

Jesus got up out of that grave on Sunday morning! All power, all power was in His hands. Let me tell you today, if you love my Jesus, you ought to know Him. You ought to have some power. Oh, bless His name. When they lie about you, you ought to have some power. When you get sick in your body, you ought to have some get-up power. You ought to have power to tell the world, "I'm a true worshiper of Jesus Christ."

Thank You, Lord. Oh, I thank You, Lord. Glory to God, I feel it now! I feel it now, moving on the inside of me. Let me tell you that Jesus, the mighty Lamb of God — oh, bless His name, I feel it now — nobody can do you like the Lord! Nobody! Let me tell you this morning, many folks don't want to hear about it. They want use everything else as a way of doing things, but nobody can do you like the Lord! Nobody can do you like Jesus. I'm glad! I'm glad I can call on Him.

I'm trying to close, here. I can hear Brother Abernathy saying, "Go on. One day you're going to hear about me. I don't want you to worry."

Oh, glory to God. I pray I've left you with Something that will lead you and guide you. Maybe you have not accepted the Lord as your personal Savior. I've got to tell the world today, "the wages of sin is death, but the gift of God is eternal life." We need to start telling people, "if you don't get it right, Jesus might come and catch you with your works undone."

If you're here this morning, and you've never accepted Jesus as your personal Savior, you can come now. I want to tell you today, maybe you've been trying to get close to Jesus, and you've tried everything, and nothing works. But it's something about being a true worshiper of Jesus Christ. You ought to feel something. You ought to know you've been washed in the blood of the Lamb.

I'm glad that Jesus has raised me up. If you're here this morning and you need a closer walk with the Lord, true worship is calling on Him, calling on His holy name. Thank You, Jesus. Thank You, Jesus. Thank You, Jesus!

If you're here this morning, and the Spirit of God is dealing with you, you can come now. Somebody may say this morning, "There's no reason for me to come." Well, let me tell you today, we all need power. Let me tell you this morning: much prayer, much power; little prayer, little power; no prayer, no power. If you're not praying today, let me tell you what you are missing. It's like having a cake with no icing on it. You can pray. You can call on Him today. He'll move in every situation. Thank You, Lord. Oh, bless His name today.

The Lord is moving in a mighty way. Thank You, Lord. There's something about Jesus, we can call on Him. We can call on Him. Call His name today.

A Song of Comfort
Psalm 23

Would you turn in your Bibles this morning, to the book of Psalms? The 23rd chapter of Psalms today. Turn with me to that book in the Old Testament, Psalm 23.

Let me ask you this. How many of you have your Bibles? Amen. Can we have a Bible count? In other words, we want folks to know who we're witnessing for. Amen? If you walk out of your house and you don't have anything but a Playboy magazine, people know what you're doing. But when you walk out your door with your Bible, the devil knows you've got the Word of God. For the Bible says, only the Word of God will stand. Heaven and earth will pass away, but the Word of God will stand forever.

Let's start with this young man. Let me put a Bible in his hand. This is how to train your children, mothers. Put a Bible in his hand, the Word of God in his hand. Put it in their hands, because if we don't put something in their hands, as a Christian organization, the world will put something in their hands and their mouths too, and anything else the devil will try.

Psalm 23 this morning is where our message is coming from. We ask you to read along with us. Would you read along with me this morning?

1. The Lord is my shepherd; I shall not want.
2. He maketh me to lie down in green pastures: he leadeth me beside the still waters.
3. He restoreth my soul: he leadeth me in the paths of righteousness for his name's sake.
4. Yea, though I walk through the valley of the shadow of death, I will fear no evil: for thou art with me; thy rod and thy staff they comfort me.
5. Thou preparest a table before me in the presence of mine enemies: thou anointest my head with oil; my cup runneth over.
6. Surely goodness and mercy shall follow me all the days of my life: and I will dwell in the house of the Lord for ever.

Let us pray at this time.

My Father, we come to You this morning, Lord God. We pray now that You would anoint the Word. Oh, heavenly Father, not my will, but Thy will be done. Oh, heavenly Father, use these lips of clay, Lord God, that I might say a Word for You. Oh, heavenly Father, we pray for the ones sitting in the pews today. Open up our eyes, Lord God. Open up our ears, that we not only will be a hearer, but a doer of the Word. Oh, Lord God, You have been good to us, and You've brought us from a mighty long way. We magnify Your name today. We glorify Your name, for Your name is worthy to be praised. We lift You up today, Lord God, for there is power in Your name: wonder-working power, miracle-working power, saving power, in the name of Jesus.

There's nothing too hard for You today, Lord God. You have more medicine in the hem of Your garment than any drugstore in the land. You've got more power, Lord God, than a nuclear bomb, and we praise You today. Oh, heavenly Father, as we look to You today, we're asking You to have Your way; not our will but Your will be done. In Jesus' name we pray, amen, amen, amen.

I want to talk for a few minutes from that 23rd Psalm today, "A Song of Comfort." Would you say that with me this morning? "A song of comfort." When I think about something as being a comfort, I think about a water bed. It has a comforter on it. It has a temperature of being always the same, a comfort. But we're talking about a different kind of comfort today, a song of comfort.

We were talking this morning about some of the songs that we hear today, and we agreed that a lot of those songs don't have any depth in them. We hear them this month, and then they are gone next month. We hear about the artist for while, and then do not hear about them anymore. But there's something about the songs of old, something about that song 'Amazing Grace, how sweet the sound, that saved a wretch like me.' There's something about those songs. They had meaning to them. And we can rejoice in the fact today that God truly is in control. You ought to have a song in your heart. Everywhere you go, there ought to be something that you can pull out from within. It ought to give you strength for the next round of whatever you're dealing with.

I'm glad that I have a song this morning. I don't know all the words to it. It's something about when my burdens get heavy, I can feel that song within my heart, and I can feel the wheel begin to turn inside of me. There's something about that song, that when things don't go like they should, I don't have to steal away, but it's something within. When I think about it, it brings joy to my heart. It brings a smile to my face. It does something to my mind the world can't do, and the world can't take it away.

I'm talking about a song of comfort this morning. It is the duty of Christians to encourage themselves in the Lord their God. It's your duty as a Christian to know that your hope and trust don't come from man. It is your duty as a Christian to know that your house is not built on sinking sand. Your house should be built on a rock, so when the storms of life begin to come, you are able to stand. We ought to take encouragement from that.

There was a time when David was a shepherd. There's only one good Shepherd, and that is Jesus Christ. I don't care what men tell you, I don't care what women tell you, but Jesus said, "My sheep hear and know My voice." I don't know about you today, but Jesus is calling right now. It wasn't the message that drew the young man, but it's something about knowing the Shepherd, knowing the One who sits high, the One who looks low. And we see this morning, this is the shepherd's responsibility. He who is the Shepherd of Israel is the Shepherd of every individual believer. He takes them into His fold, and then He takes care of them. He protects them and provides for them, with more care than any other shepherd can. His business is tending and taking care of His flock.

I heard the testimonies this morning of ones saying how God worked it out, not how or when they wanted it worked out, but in His own way and His own time. God is always right on time. I'm glad this morning that I can lift Him up. I can praise His name. It should not be your will, but it ought to be God's will, in every way, in everything you want to do.

I want to tell you this morning that many people are going through hell because they are not where God wants them to be. But when you are where He wants you to be, you have a joy that the world can't give. You have a peace that passes all understanding. Oh, I'm glad this morning that I can praise His name. I don't know about you this morning, but you ought to have a song down on the inside. You ought to have a joy that the world didn't give, and the world can't take away. I don't mean from crack smoking. I don't mean from alcohol. I don't mean from lying and gossiping. I mean from knowing who your Savior is, who your Shepherd is. You ought to have something on the inside.

Every now and then, when your burdens get heavy, you ought to know Somebody. I know Somebody, Somebody by the name of Jesus. Nobody can do you like the Lord. I love the Lord. He is my true Shepherd. Is He your Shepherd today? Does He lead you? Does He guide you into all truth and righteousness? You can call on His name. In His name, there's power. Whatever you need today, you can call on His name. He might not come when you want Him, but He's always right on time.

As a believer today, you ought to have confidence in God, for it says in the 23rd Psalm, "I shall not want." Let me tell you this morning, maybe things don't go like you think they should, but you should not want. You ought to thank the Lord for all things. Thank the Lord for the storms of life. Thank the Lord — glory to God — when things are good. Paul said, "I rejoice in all things, whatsoever, I rejoice." Job said, "Though You slay me, Lord, yet will I serve You."

I feel the Spirit moving on the inside of me. I'm glad. I'm glad today! I know my God. I know my Redeemer. He lives. And where does He live? He lives inside of me.

As a believer, you ought to have confidence. Let not those fears stagger you. Let not those fears that the devil would say take you away from God. The Lord is in control, not only of heaven, but He's in control of this earth. You ought to rejoice today, for the Word of God has to be fulfilled. You ought to feel comforted with a song moving down on the inside.

Let me move on here today. The courage of a dying saint, the superstition of eminent danger. "Though I walk through the valley of the shadow of death, I will fear no evil, for Thou art with me." A believer may meet death with a holy security and security of the mind, because there is no evil in it for the saints of God. I told my lodge brothers last night, "They're fighting for gold in this country and in this world, but the saints of God are going to walk on the streets of gold."

I'm glad about that today. I don't have to worry, because God will supply my needs, according to His riches in glory, through His Son, Jesus Christ. I'm glad! I'm glad today.

As I move on this morning, look to God, a significant Supplier of all your needs. It says in Psalm 23, "Thou preparest a table before me." It may be beans and bread, but God has a table prepared for all of those who know Him, who have called on His holy name.

He's a plentiful Supplier today. What you need, my God has it. Not what you want, but what you need, my God has it. Seek the Lord while He may be found. Seek the Lord. Put your hand in God's hands, and He will make a way out of no way. He will turn your midnights into day. He will prepare a table before us in the presence of our enemies.

He goes on to say, "Thou anointest my head with oil. My cup runneth over." Let me tell you this morning, your cup ought to be running over, running over with the love of the Lord. I tell the world, everywhere I go, "I know Jesus will make a way for me. I know Jesus can heal my body. I know Jesus can turn my midnights into day." You ought to know He is the Supplier of all your needs. And then he goes on to say, "Surely goodness and mercy shall follow me." His pardoning mercy, His protecting mercy, His sustaining mercy, His supplying mercy. I'm glad this morning.

As I move on here, he goes on to say, "all the days of my life." He shall follow us even to the last. For whom God loves, He loves even to the end. He loves you so much that He sent His darling Son, Jesus. I'm glad today, I can call on Him. I'm glad He looked beyond my faults, and He saw my needs. I'm glad I've got a foundation that's built on the rock, the rock of Jesus. I feel like preaching now! Oh, bless His name! There's something about the Word of God. Sometimes I find myself preaching to my own self. Some of the sermons on tapes, I find myself preaching to myself saying, "Jesus, I needed that. Jesus, not my will." Can you tell somebody, "Not my will, Lord, but Thy will be done?"

As I move on here, "I will dwell in the house of the Lord," not just one day, but I'm going to dwell there forever. Here's a prospect of perfection of bliss in the future state, something to stand. That means God's goodness and mercy have followed me all the days of my life on this earth, and when this life is ended, I shall move on to a better world. I want to tell you this morning, we're in the land of the dying, getting ready for the land of living. I'm not living over here. Every time I look in the mirror, I see myself dying. Every time I read the newspaper, I hear about people dying. But we're going to live on the other side. The only way is Jesus' way. There is no other way.

A man told me the other day, "Reverend, I can't believe God would condemn a person to eternal damnation." I said, "Brother, the Word says that there was a rich man and a man named Lazarus. And the Word says that the rich man died and he went to hell." But let me tell you this morning, God didn't condemn him. He made his own decision. You can make your own decision. You can believe in the Lord and serve Him and go to heaven. You can stand on His Word, oh, glory to God, and reign with the saints of God.

I'm glad this morning. I know the Lord. He's been good. Somebody was saying, "He has been better than good." You can call on His holy name. Stand on His Word.

As I close this morning, look at Jesus hanging on the cross, blood running down from His hands and His feet. But He didn't say a mumbling word. He just said, "Father, forgive them, for they know not what they do." Can you tell somebody, "You've done me wrong but I can forgive you, because of Jesus, who died for me." How can I say I love God, whom I've never seen, if I have no love for anybody else? You ought to have that real love down on the inside.

His arms stretched out wide, blood running down His hands and His feet, but He didn't say a mumbling word. He died for your sins. He died for my sins. He died for the sins of the world. Look at Jesus this morning, His head hanging down, hanging down for your sins, hanging down for my sins. They took Him down and they placed Him in a borrowed tomb. That lets me know that one day, this body is going back to the dust, but it's not going to stay there.

The Word says He lay down on that Friday night. He lay down. Saturday, He was still down. The Word says, on Sunday morning, something began to happen. If Jesus hadn't got up, I would have no reason to preach His name. I would have no reason for lifting Him up. But He did! He got up! As He lay there in that tomb, I can see angels coming down from heaven. I can see them rolling that big, old stone away. It was a big stone. No one man could move it. They rolled the stone away. It wasn't a man that rolled it. It wasn't the soldiers that rolled it. But let me tell you, the messengers of God, they rolled the stone away. Thank You, Jesus! They rolled the stone away.

And the Word says that morning, that resurrection morning, when they rolled the stone away, Jesus got up. I can just imagine Jesus: He didn't just jump up like so many of us do, but He got up. I can see Jesus getting up. He probably sat there on the side of His grave. He sat there for a few minutes, and He said, "Father, I thank You." And the Word says, He got all the way up. He got out of His grave clothes. He laid them down, and the Word says, He got up with all power in His hands.

You ought to have some power. You ought to be able to stand and say, "Jesus," or get on your knees and say, "Jesus, I can't make it by myself. I can't make it by myself, but I can make it with God's grace. I can make it with my hands in God's hands." Let me tell you this morning, you ought to have some getting-up power.

Jesus got on that cloud. He went all the way back to glory. I'm glad that He sent me Something He said would lead me and guide me. He sent me power, not Black or White power, but Holy Ghost power. He sent me love, and it didn't come as part-time love. He sent me joy that didn't just come when the liquor stores are open. He sent me Something that would give me a song to sing. He sent me Something that would be a Mother for me. He sent me Something to be a Father for me. I'm glad! I'm glad, Jesus, that You went on that cloud. I'm glad, Jesus, that You went away, and I'm glad You sent the Comforter, the Holy Ghost, that You promised would lead us and guide us into all truth and righteousness.

The Word says, "Come as you are." This morning, come as you are, and God will make a way out of no way. I'm glad that God is in control. Jesus said, "Unless you come as little children, you will otherwise never be able to enter in." Come to Him with a child-like attitude.

Many of us put things in the way of God. You might say this morning, "I don't have a husband," but what about your automobile? What about your furniture? What about your house? Some of us have jobs we put before the Lord. Why do you think many aren't being blessed? I'm talking about Christians today, who aren't blessed in the Lord. They put something else before the Lord. But let me tell you today, my God is a jealous God. Oh, bless His name today.

God wants you to come to Him. You can come now. Somebody will say this morning, "I don't need a church." But we're living in a time when everybody needs somebody. Everybody needs a praying Christian on his side. Everybody needs a prayer partner. When things are not going the way they should, you need to have somebody you can call on. You need to be able to say, "I want you to pray with me. Pray for me that the Lord's will be done."

Come to Jesus, just as you are. If you're wounded, if you're lonely, you can find in Him a resting place, and He will make you glad. If you're here this morning, you need to come now. Come to Jesus. Come to Jesus.

In His Own Image
Genesis 2:21-25

I have learned to depend upon His Word. Through it all, sometimes up, and sometimes down, I've learned to depend upon His Word. Oh, glory to His name! I could shout all over this little building right now. Oh, bless His name today!

We are grateful to God for each of you this morning. I want to get right into the message. Would you turn in your Bibles with me to the book of Genesis, the second chapter of Genesis this morning, beginning at the 21st verse. The question is asked, "Is there a Word from the Lord?" There's always a Word from God. Amen. We are just grateful to God this morning, for another day that He has given us to lift up His holy name. For the Word tells us, if He be lifted up, He would draw all men.

In the second chapter of Genesis this morning, beginning at the 21st verse, there is a Word from the Lord today. We are grateful to God for what He has done, for what the Lord is doing, and for what He's going to do in the service. I'm mindful today that the Word tells us that faith comes by hearing and hearing by the Word of God. And how can we hear without a preacher? And how can they preach unless they be sent? Before we get into the Word of God, let us open up with a word of prayer.

Oh, gracious Father, we come to You this morning, and Lord God, we come as an empty vessel before a full fountain. Oh, heavenly Father, we know You're able to fill these empty vessels this morning. We pray, Lord God, that You would move and get self out of the way, that Thy will, which is perfect, would be done. Oh, heavenly Father, as we come to You this morning, we come standing on Your Word today. Oh, Lord God, You've been good to us. We're not begging today, but we are asking in Your name, for we know, Lord God, that You're everywhere at the same time.

Oh, heavenly Father, we know that You are an all-hearing God, an all-seeing God. We come, Lord God, asking You right now, in the name of Jesus, that You would have Your way. Oh, Lord God, have Your way. I ask that You would use me in a mighty way. Oh, heavenly Father, we thank You today. We thank You, heavenly Father. We know that You're in control of every situation. Now, Lord, have Your way today, in the name of Jesus, for there's power in that name, wonder working power, healing power, delivering power, in the name of Jesus. Now, Lord, we pray that the Spirit of God that is in this place would go beyond these four walls, and go out into the hedges and highways, out where sin is raging. Oh, heavenly Father, have Your way today. Not our will, but let Thy will be done.

Oh, heavenly Father, we need You right now. We're standing today, in the name of Jesus. Your name, Lord God, there's power in your name: all power, today, not white power, not black power, but Holy Ghost power; power that will make us love our enemies, power that will make us do right. Power, Lord God, that will be with us on our dying day. Thank You, Jesus, for Holy Ghost power. Thank You, Jesus, for saving power today.

Now, Lord, one day, praying days will be over. One day, our coming together like this will be over, but You've got a place for us. Oh, glory to Your name. There's saving power in Your name. Over there, Lord God, You've got a mansion for us, and we thank You for it right now. Thank You, Jesus, for what You're going to do right now. Thank You, Jesus! Oh, bless Your name today! Oh, bless Your name! Your name, Lord God, there's something about Your name. Your name can cool a scorching fever. Your name can heal a sin-sick soul. Oh, bless Your name today. Your name, Lord God, there's power in Your name. Now, Lord, help us today. Help us today, to say a Word for You. Thank You, Jesus. Thank You, Lord, for what You're going to do, in Jesus' name. Thank God. Thank God. Thank God.

In the book of Genesis this morning, the second chapter, the 21st verse, would you read along with us?

21. And the Lord caused a deep sleep to fall upon Adam, and he slept: and he took one of his ribs and closed the flesh instead thereof;
22. And the rib, which the Lord God had taken from man, made he a woman, and brought her unto the man.
23. And Adam said, this is now bone of my bones, and flesh of my flesh: she shall be called Woman, because she was taken out of Man.
24. Therefore shall a man leave his father and his mother, and shall cleave unto his wife: and they shall be one flesh.

25. And they were both naked, the man and his wife, and were not ashamed.

May God bless the reader and hearer of His holy Word.

The other day a woman asked me, "What is a mother?" I said to her, "Just about any woman can have a baby, but it takes a special woman to be a mother." I want to preach to you this morning about the first mother, Eve. I have often thought to myself about Adam and Eve, that they were born as men and women, with everything that God had given them. They weren't born as children. They were born full-grown.

I want to talk about this morning, the thought of the subject, "In His Own Image." Would you say that with me today? "In His Own Image." You may say, "That is a very different kind of subject on such a day as today." But I'm grateful to God this morning, as I've mentioned earlier, that there are a lot of people having babies, but there are not many mothers today. I am mindful this morning, there are 50- and 60-year-old women who have had babies, and you better not call them mothers. I had a lady come to me last year, she was way up in her 70's. I asked her, "How are you doing, Mother?" And she told me, "I am not a mother."

Well, I'm mindful this morning that only God can make a mother. You might say this morning, "What about society? What about the ones who go through all of these things, giving birth?" Only God can make a mother.

The story of the first woman begins with Eve in the Garden of Eden, where she discovered that she bore a unique relationship to God, the supreme Power in the universe. The great reality is not that she came from the rib of Adam, but that God created her, and brought her womanly nature into being.

The divine purpose relative to woman is found in the first part of the story of creation.

Genesis 1:27: "So God created man in His own image, in the image of God created he him: male and female created he them."

Here we have warrant for woman's dominion. The fact that God did not give man dominion until he had woman standing beside him is evidence of her exalted place in creation. Various theories regarding the origin of Genesis and of the story concerning Eve, the first woman, have been evolved. Some scholars believe that parts of

Genesis are based upon myths and fables. Others call it a legend wrapped around fundamental spiritual truths.

All Bible scholars concede that the start of creation was conceived by an ancient Person to whom great truths about the spiritual universe in which they lived were becoming known. How these truths became known and why, scholars cannot answer.

I believe the Word of God. God said it, and I believe it. Somebody said, "What the Bible says, that tells it right there."

The magnificent thing about the story is that God, seeing the incompleteness of man standing alone, wanted to find a helper for him. Not having found this helper in all other created things, such as the birds of the air or the beasts of the field, God was obliged to make for man an helper, who was his equal, and who shared in the same process of creation in which he shared. And so God created this helper, Eve, whose name means life, not from the animal kingdom, but from the rib of Adam himself. The symbolism of the rib is that it was taken from the place nearest to Adam's heart, indicating the close relationship of man and woman. The real answer to the story is that man and woman were made for each other, that woman is bone of his bone and flesh of his flesh. Therefore, they were not all that God intended them to be until they were together.

The oneness of man and woman in true marriage comes into its fullest means in Genesis 2:24.

"Therefore shall a man leave his father and his mother, and shall cleave unto his wife: and they shall be one flesh."

Marriage emerged at that time, not as a civil contract, but as a divine instruction. In this union of Adam and Eve, all marriage becomes congealed, and with creation finally demonstrating that the laws of Eve herself, like all of us, came into a universe that was invariably disorderly. Oh, we can see this morning, it wasn't man, but it was God, all by Himself.

In the Genesis account, Eve is elevated to ethical beauty and lasting dignity. As a great sculptor might strike a figure out of marble, we can see that she was a beautiful creation. She was a creation that God had created in all of His wealth. I'm mindful this morning that you women, as I look around today, you each look so beautiful. I'm glad that there are still Christian women who are standing on the wall. I'm glad there are Christian women who are still praying, who can get a prayer through. There's something about a woman's prayer that makes a difference. Let me tell you this morning, there's something about a mother's prayer.

I can remember a few years ago, when I needed a mother's prayer. I called my mother in Detroit, and she began to talk with me about when I was born, and even before that time. I'm glad, this morning, that I have a mother who is still alive. Some of you, your mothers have gone on to glory.

But let me tell you this morning, Jesus said He will be a mother for you. I wish I could tell others who have lost their mothers, "You don't have to worry, for Jesus said, 'Don't worry, I'll be with you all the way. I'll be with you until the end of time.' "

Of all the great women we know of today, there's something special about Mother Eve. When she listened to the serpent, representing temptation, she followed not the will of God, but she followed the path of evil, when she ate the first fruit from the forbidden tree. She acted independently of God, in whose image she had been created, from God who watched over her. Her interest turned to a serpent, which distorted the truth, regarding the fruit God had forbidden them to eat. The serpent beguiled Eve by telling her if she would eat of the forbidden fruit, she would gain for herself a new delight.

Everything you want is not always good. Let me tell you this morning, you ought to know today that God is in control. Somebody asked me the other week, "What about God's will?" I said, "Before you start talking about God's will, see what the Word of God has to say It has to be in line with the Word of God." I'm glad for the Word of God, for Jesus said, "Heaven and earth will pass away, but the Word of God will stand forever." We can call upon the name of the Lord.

After Eve had partaken of the forbidden fruit, she also gave it to Adam, and he, too, ate, also sharing in her guilt. In this act, we have an excellent example of woman's imprudence and man's inclination to follow woman wherever she leads, even into sin. Eve with Adam hid from the presence of God, for they knew they had done wrong. Let me tell you this morning, I don't have to look into your windows and watch all these kinds of things. The Lord sits high, and He looks low. I'm glad this morning.

Afterwards, when Eve told God that the serpent beguiled her and she'd eaten the fruit, she displayed the natural tendency of people, to blame not herself for her own wrongdoings, but those around her. You might say, "I've been guilty." But everybody I know of, or I can think of, that's locked up downtown or in any other jail, they're always blaming somebody else for their own sinful deeds. You ought to be able, if you have done somebody wrong, to go and tell that person, "I'm sorry, I have done you wrong." That's real love.

Oh, glory to God. The Word says, "If a man say, I love God, and hateth his brother, he is a liar: for he that loveth not his brother whom he hath seen, how can he love God whom he hath not seen?" The Word says you are a liar, and no liar will enter the kingdom of God. I'm glad for the example that I have, in the Word. Somebody would say, every person in the Word of God is an example that we too are human beings. But my God is in control. You can call on Him no matter what your circumstances may be.

I'm glad this morning, as I move on here, for Jesus, the mighty Lamb of God. In the birth of the first son, Cain, and the second son, Abel, Eve experienced all types of pain of childbirth, never forgetting what God had said after she ate of the forbidden fruit: "I will multiply your pain in childbirth." Let me tell you this morning, I believe if we didn't have so much dope given to some of these young girls that are having babies, let them experience the pain of having a child, I don't believe that they would make the same mistake two and three times. Oh, I know I'm right about that.

When the first son was born, we know that Eve, like all mothers, experienced great joy. And she said, "I have gotten a man from the Lord." Eve called her first son 'Cain,' meaning 'gotten' or 'acquired.' Eve realized that her child came, not from her flesh, but from God himself. Her positive assertion of this makes us certain that God, and not the serpent, now ruled over her life. Later Eve gave birth to a second son. And his name was Abel, meaning 'breath,' or 'fading away.' The first mother saw her sons grow up to be different in nature and in interest, and later she discerned signs of jealousy between the two boys. I want to tell you this morning, if you have kids today, you better be careful.

We baptized a 12-year-old last Sunday, and I made a public statement that that young boy won't have to worry about gang activity. That young boy won't have to worry about what the world is doing. But let me tell you today, you ought to have Jesus on the inside, in your home. You ought to tell your family, "I know Jesus can make away for you."

Oh, glory to God. I'm glad this morning. I was raised in a saved home. I said, 'a saved home.' Oh, glory to God. My father would always say, "I didn't just send them to church, but I took them to church." That made a difference in my life. It's made a difference in what I've been going through. I know the Lord is a way-maker. I know the Lord is a burden bearer.

We are made in His image, yet Eve knew that God was still in this universe, which He had created in a few days. She was to see the fulfillment of His plan in her own life. Cain married, and Eve had grandchildren. A long interim elapsed. Adam, we are told, was 130 years old, and Eve couldn't have been much younger when she gave birth to Seth, his name meaning 'to appoint,' or 'to be established.' She took courage in the fact, for she said, "God has appointed me another seed instead of Abel, whom Cain slew." A great seed, she said, he was to be, for the ancestry of Jesus Christ was traced back to the line of Seth. Other sons and daughters were born to Adam and Eve, though they weren't listed. After her time of childbearing passed, Eve's story merged into that of her children, for she lived on in the life of Seth. In the stories of the children in the line of Seth's descendents, we see the name of the Lord being called.

I'm glad today. We can call upon the name of Jesus. Let me tell you this morning, we ought to be wrapped up and tied up in the Lord. We are made in His image today. Let me tell you this morning, not so much naturally so, but spiritually so, I'm in His image today. Everywhere I go, I've got to tell somebody, "I've been born again. I've been washed in the blood of the Lamb." Oh, glory to God! I'm glad this morning. Oh, bless His name today!

Let me tell you this morning, put your hand in God's hands, and He will make away out of no way. Oh, glory to God! I'm glad this morning! I can call on His name. I'm glad this morning. I can stand on His Word today. I'm glad this morning. Oh, bless His name today. I can tell the world, Jesus, the mighty Lamb of God, Jesus, is a way-maker. Jesus is in my heart. I'm glad this morning. You can stand on His Word!

As I move on here, the reason the world is in the condition that it is, some of us are not witnessing for the Lord. Everywhere you go, you ought to tell somebody, "I know the Lord. He has been good to me. I know the Lord has brought me from a mighty long way." I feel my help now. Oh, bless His name. We are made in the image of God, and we can stand on His Word.

Thank You, Lord, for what You're doing. Thank You, Lord, for what You are going to do. Oh, bless His name today.

Look at Jesus, hanging there on that cross, blood running down from His hands and His feet. He never said a mumbling word, but, "Father, oh, Father, forgive them, for they know not what they do." I'm glad this morning. You can stand on the Word of God. Look at Jesus hanging there, blood running down from His hands and His feet. He died for the sins of the world. He died for us so we might have life. He died for us, so we might have life and live in Him. Oh, bless His name today.

Are you born, not in the image of your mother and father, but reborn in the image of God? Nicodemus went to Jesus by night, and he said to Jesus, "Master, I've heard all about You. Master, I've heard about Your works. How can I be born again?" And Jesus said, "You've got to be born, not of the water, but of the Spirit." You've got to be born in the image of God. I'm glad this morning. I'm glad I'm born again, in the image of Him, my Savior. I'm glad today. We can stand on His Word.

Look at Jesus. They took Him down off that cross. They placed Him in that borrowed tomb, and all day Saturday, and all night Saturday night, He lay there. But the Word says, messengers of God went down, and they rolled the stone away. And when they rolled it away, my Jesus, my Jesus got up with all power. He had all power, all power, all power in His hand! Hallelujah! I'm glad today! He got on that cloud, and He went all the way back to glory. I'm glad, I'm glad! He went to prepare a place for me. He went all the way back to glory. He said in His Word, "In My Father's house, there are many mansions. If this were not so, I would have told you." One day I'm going to have to leave this place, but I'm going to go a little bit higher. Thank You, Lord. Thank You, Lord! And Jesus said, "If I don't go, It won't come." What won't come? Something that will lead me and guide me, and make me love my enemies.

What would come? That which would make me do right. What would come? That which would be with me. What would come? Oh, glory to God. When I want to get mad, It won't let me get mad. What will come? When they talk about me, I won't talk back. What will come? That which will make me love everybody. What will come? When things seem impossible, what will come? That which will help me.

I must testify now. I was brought up in a Baptist church all my life, and that's all I knew. A few years ago, let me tell you what happened. I went to the mountaintop, and I had a little talk with

Jesus. Before that, I let others talk for me. But then I had a little talk with the Lord, and He made everything all right. He gave me joy, way down on the inside. He put running in my feet, and He put a song in my heart. He put a testimony within me, that nobody treats me like Jesus.

I'm glad today. I'm glad He sent the Holy Spirit, that He said would lead us and guide us into all truth and righteousness.

If you're here this morning, and the Spirit of God is dealing with you, He's trying to do something in your life that will make a difference. Let me tell you this morning, nobody can treat you like the Lord. Nobody can treat you like Jesus. Nobody else can turn midnights into days. Nobody else, this morning. We are made in the image of God.

Come to Jesus.

The Eyes of the Lord
Isaiah 1:15-20

Isaiah 1:15. And when ye spread forth your hands, I will hide mine eyes from you: yea, when ye make many prayers, I will not hear: your hands are full of blood.
16. Wash you, make you clean; put away the evil of your doings from before mine eyes; cease to do evil;
17. Learn to do well; seek judgment, relieve the oppressed, judge the fatherless, plead for the widow.
18. Come now, and let us reason together, saith the Lord: though your sins be as scarlet, they shall be as white as snow; though they be red like crimson, they shall be as wool.
19. If ye be willing and obedient, ye shall eat the good of the land:
20. But if ye refuse and rebel, ye shall be devoured with the sword: for the mouth of the Lord hath spoken it.

May God bless the reader and hearer of His holy Word. I want to take from that 16th of verse as it reads this morning,

"Wash you, make you clean; put away the evil of your doings from before mine eyes; cease to do evil."

I want to talk about this morning, "The Eyes of the Lord." I was afraid this morning, when Mother Watkins was witnessing and testifying to us today about how God was looking out for her, she had touched upon the message today, because she just really hit a home run for Jesus this morning. We're grateful to God, because where else could you have been, where you could hear a testimony like that? I don't know of any TV programs where you can hear a testimony like that. Maybe that might be something we ought to start having, live testimonies on TV for the goodness of God. I believe we could be strengthened by those testimonies, as we've heard this morning.

From the subject, "The Eyes of the Lord," God sees our sinning and our failure. God sees our sinking down, and he sees our unkindness, our love for our own concepts and our deceits, our travailings. Behind all our illusions, God sees our iniquity. I was thinking this morning, and when Mother said she was lying there on the ground, I don't know how long she lay there, but it must've been a while. But God saw that and He saw the perfect time that someone would come by and respond to her need. I'm grateful to God today. He may not come when you want Him, but He's always right on time. You may think you need Him right now. You may think your burdens are so heavy that you can't go another step. Well, let me tell you this morning, sisters and brothers, God knows, and He cares. And not only does He know and care, but He sees all things. He sits high, and He looks low.

It says in the 16th verse, He placed into the mouth of Isaiah these words, "Wash you and make you clean." Then He says, "put away the evil of your doings from before mine eyes." But no man can put away his doings, whether they be good or bad, from before the eyes of Jehovah. I want to tell you this morning, regardless of what's happening in the world today, God knows, and He cares. I am a living witness this morning. I can hide from you, but I can't hide from God. We can see this morning what He was saying, and what He meant when He said, "Stop what you're doing." Toss those intents, toss those motives, toss those egos. Put them away from you. Take them and cast them away from you. Cast away the lust from you. Cast away the pride from you. Cast away the envy from you. He says to cast it from you and put it in a sea of forgetfulness where it will never rise again.

I am thankful this morning for the story of David. The Word says David was a man who loved God, a man God called after His own heart. There was situation that David was caught up in, and the story says Nathan, the man of God, went to King David and told him that in the kingdom where David was the king, there was a situation where a man was doing some things contrary to the law of God. Then Nathan said to King David, "King, what do you think we ought to do about it?"

King David said to the man of God, "That man, whoever he is doing that thing, he ought to be beheaded. He ought to be put in chains. He ought to be put in the lions' den. He ought to be crucified and his life ought to be taken away." Then the king said to the prophet, "Who is this man?"

And Nathan said, "Oh, King, you are that man."

You may be able to hide from someone else, but you can't hide from God. Oh, I'm thankful to the Lord this morning, the eyes of the Lord are upon this world. Let nobody tell you that they are getting away with anything. I know some people right now who are on their bed of affliction. God is just gripping them and He won't let them go because they have to give an account, not only on the other side, but on this side as well. When one of the sisters used to take care of an elderly man a few years ago, I can remember this elderly man saying, "Tell the Pastor to pray for me because I want to die." Let me tell you this morning, the eyes of the Lord are upon every one of us, and we're not going to leave here until the Lord calls us home. We're not going to leave here, regardless of what we might want to do. The Lord is in control.

Let me tell you this morning, as I move on here today, King David said, "I know I'm the man. I'm the man, and what choice do I have?" Men will do you any kind of way, but only God can give you justice. For the man of God said to King David, "The Lord has spoken to me and told me to tell you, you're going to have to give an account." We're going to have to give an account of our deeds and our misdeeds.

I want to tell you this morning that time is winding down. It's shorter than we think. Somebody said the other day, "Do you know when Jesus is coming?" I want to tell you, no man knows the day or the hour when the Lord is coming. But Jesus said that when you see these signs, mothers against fathers, and fathers against sons, and children and kids being raped, seems like every day, when you see these things, the time is not nigh, but it's getting closer to the end time. No man knows the day or the hour when the Lord is coming. But I want to tell you today, you ought to be ready when the Lord comes. Not getting ready, but be ready, when He comes. The Lord ought to come and find you working in the vineyard, and then He is going to reward you according to your works.

I told somebody the other day that I felt within my soul, I will never retire from the ministry of Jesus Christ. I will never give up. Oh, glory to God. In some professions, after 30 years, they leave their jobs and go home and sit down. Men in some professions are happy to make money, then they go home and sit down. But when you have the gospel plow, you have told the Lord "I'll sell out for You, and wherever You lead me, I'll go. I'll go for You, Lord, and whatever You want me to do, I will do for You, Lord." I may not feel good sometimes, as Mother Watkins has said, but let me tell you this morning, you should say, "I'll go for You, Lord, morning, noon, and night. I'll go for You, Jesus, when I don't feel good. I'll go for You, Jesus, oh, glory to God, when I don't have a way." But let me tell you this morning, one day we're going to be rewarded, not like man would do. I'm just like Mother today. I don't want my reward down here, where men can steal it and moths can corrupt it. But I want my reward — oh, glory to God, the eyes of the Lord are upon us right now — I want my reward (oh, bless His name) in heaven! Oh, thank You, Jesus.

I say all the time, "We're fighting for gold down here. Gold prices are going up. But on the other side, oh, bless His name, we're going to walk the streets of gold." Thank You, Jesus. Oh, thank You, Lord. No inflation on the other side. No more sickness on the other side. No more darkness on the other side. There's going to be peace. Oh, glory to God. There's going to be love on the other side. I'm glad today, for the eyes of the Lord are upon me right now. The eyes of the Lord are upon the world. The eyes of the Lord are on every one of us, and I'm glad! I'm glad! I'm glad this morning! I can call on His name. I'm glad I've got a God that's got all power, not a little g-o-d, but a big God that's got the whole world in His hands! I'm glad this morning! Everywhere you go, you ought to tell somebody, "I know the Lord is good. I know the Lord has brought me from a mighty long way." I'm glad this morning.

Let me tell you today, the race is not given to the swiftest nor to the strongest, but to those that hold out, and endure until the end. I want ask you this morning, will you hold out until the end? Will you hold out in the race?

As I move on here today, oh, glory to God, David said, "If I'm given a choice by God, I don't want to be put in the hands of man, because I know man will talk about you. I know man will put you down. I know man will never forget what you have done five, ten, fifteen or twenty years ago. I know man will always want to bring it up." David said, "I know I have to give an account. I don't want to be in the hands of men." And then Nathan told David, "Well, what about nature?" (If you've noticed, we've had 5 showers in the last two hours.)

David said, "I do not want to be put in the hands of nature, because nature has no limitations." (Look at Mount St. Helens, it blew ten years ago this week.) So let me tell you today, God is in control. David said, "I know I've got to make a decision, because the eyes of the Lord are on me right now. I know I've got to make a decision about what I have done." The Spirit said, "David, why don't you put your life in God's hands?" And David said, "I know who my Redeemer is." It's Jesus, all the way. Put your life in God's hands, and everything will be all right.

40

I'm glad, for the eyes of the Lord! I'm glad, this morning! I can put my hands in His hands today! As I close this morning, Jesus is the mighty Lamb of God! Jesus, oh, bless His name! Jesus is the means by which God saves the world. Oh, bless His name today! Thank You, Lord. Oh, thank You, Lord. Jesus is all we need this morning. You can put your trust in Him.

I'm glad today! Oh, bless His name! How sweet it is to walk in the steps of the Savior, walking in the light, in the path of right. Oh, how sweet it is to walk with Jesus, to walk in His love, and to walk in His understanding. Oh, how sweet it is, to know that one day I'm going to lay this body down. Then I'm going to receive a body that will never die. I'm going to receive some eyes that are never going to go dim. Oh, glory to God. I don't know what they give out over there, but I want to get there. I want to see Jesus. Oh, bless His name, and I want to see Mother Brown there. Oh, glory to God! I'm going to tell her, "Mother Brown, would you fix me some of that corn bread?"

You ought to have somebody who's on the other side you want to follow —not follow men and all of their doings, but you ought to have somebody as an example that you can follow all the way. Mother told me just last year, "Pastor, I used to wonder about you, wonder about your salvation and wonder about where you're going." But then she said to me, "I have seen a growth in you. I have seen how God has been dealing with you, and I'm not worried about where you're going. If I get there before you do, I'll tell the Lord you are coming on one day. You're coming on up, a little bit higher. You're coming on up to be with me." I'm glad this morning, I've got Jesus on my side. I'm glad this morning. Do you have Him today? Let me see your hands today. Do you have Him all on the inside? Do you have Him? Are you tied up, tangled up, and wrapped up in the Lord?

Now we have become the sons of God. We also have become lights of the world. Jesus said, "You are the light of the world. A light that hides not under a bushel, but a light that shines." Let it shine, let it shine! Can you let your light shine? Can you let your light shine, where men will say, "I know there's a believer there. I know there's a born-again believer there." With your lights on this morning, everywhere you go will lighten with light. I say, let it shine, let it shine, in the world of darkness today. You may not always see clearly while you shine. There's a strange paradox in shining. We, unlike God, cannot know everything we see. But we'll understand it better by and by. So just because we don't understand everything we see, that doesn't mean we should shine any less. We see through a glass darkly, but then we will see Him face to face. I'm glad this morning, I'm going to see Him. I'm glad this morning, I'm going to see Jesus. I'm glad this morning, we're going to be caught up in the blood of the Lamb.

I don't know about you today, but you ought to have some get-up power. You ought to have some resurrection power. You ought to be able to say today, "I know my Redeemer. He lives today. I know Jesus will make a way out of no way." I say to you this morning, put your hands in God's hand. Don't worry about what the world says. Don't worry about what others say. Just stand on the Word. The Word of God is all you need. The Word of God will never pass away. The Word of God will stand forever.

Look at Jesus this morning, hanging on that cross, blood running down from His hands and His feet, but He didn't say a mumbling word. He died that we might have life. He died on the cross for the sins of the world. Thank You, Lord, for what You're doing. Thank You, Lord, for what You're going to do. Move by Your Spirit in a mighty way.

As I close this morning, look at Jesus. They hanged Him up on that cross. They hanged Him wide. But all He said was, "Oh, Father, forgive them, for they know not what they do." They pierced Him in His side, blood and water running together.

Can you tell somebody, "You may have done me wrong, but I forgive you." Thank You, Lord, for what You're doing right now. Look at Jesus. They brought Him down off that cross. They placed Him in that cold, dark tomb, all day Saturday and all night Saturday night. But Sunday morning, oh, glory to God, I can see the angel rolling the stone away! I can see (oh, bless His name) the angel rolling that big, old stone away! I see my Savior! One day you'll have to lay this body down. But you're going to get a new body. I see my Savior getting up out of the grave, saying, "All power, all power, not white power, not black power, but all power is in My hands." I'm glad this morning! He got up from the grave with all power!

And I see Him getting on that cloud, going all the way back, all the way back, all the way to heaven, all the way to where His Father is. Oh, glory to God! I see Him sending down, sending Something down to make a way out of no way, sending Something down that will be with you, sending Something down so when they turn off a light, it will still be on, sending Something down. When I don't understand, It ought to give understanding. When I can't see my way, It will make a way for me. Thank You, Lord, oh, thank You, Jesus, for the joy that I have, the world didn't give to me. Thank You, Lord, for the peace I have within my soul. Oh, Lord, I thank You today.

As I close this morning, I want to tell you, whatever you get, get the Lord on your side. Don't get the world, but get the Lord. Everybody's watching the Trailblazer team, but I want to tell you today, I've got Jesus in my heart. Thank You, Lord. I haven't heard if the Trailblazers give God the glory. You can have all the fortune and all the fame, but if you don't have Jesus on your side, the fortune is going to do you no good on the other side. That fame won't do you any good. Your name will be just like anybody's name, if you don't have a new name written down in glory, if you don't have a new name. I'm glad today, for the eyes of Lord. I'm glad this morning. I have my name written down in the Book of Books. Nobody can take it out. Mother's name is written in the Book of Books. Nobody can take it out.

As I close, if you're here this morning, and God is dealing with you, I want to ask you this morning to come as you are. Somebody would say, "I came to Jesus as I was. I was wounded and I was naked. I was hungry and I was sad. I was down and I was out, but I found in Him a resting place." Only in Him can you find joy. Only in Him can you find peace. Only in Him can you find fullness. I tell you today, if you have the Lord on your side, everything, everything is alright with you. Let me tell you this morning, as I am closing here, many people today want to talk about preachers or anything else, but it's Jesus who is the way-maker and the burden bearer. Nobody can get to the Father unless they come through Him.

I'm glad this morning! I found the Lord! I found Him for myself. I'm glad this morning! Oh, bless God! Every time I look around here, I think about some of my old friends. A lot of them have been killed, a lot of them have been dead for 20+ years, a lot are in jail, a lot of them are in wheelchairs, or in hospitals, but the Lord has — I could shout right through the roof! — the Lord has been good to me! He is good to every one of us who stands on His Word. If you're here this morning, and you need some get-up power, I want to pray for you right now. You can come to Jesus.

A Daring Testimony
John 9:22-31

I want to say "Thank You," to the Lord this morning, for what He has done and what He is going to do today. The Word tells us to lift Him up, and we're going to lift up the name of the Lord this morning. You might say, "What about the masses?" I want to say to you today that the way to righteousness is a narrow way, and the way to holiness is a narrow way, but the way to destruction is a broad way, and many are on that broad way. Truly we're grateful to the Lord today that we want to be on that narrow way, going right on in to where Jesus is. As we come together this morning, we know there is a Word from the Lord today, for the Bible tells us that faith comes by hearing and hearing by the Word of God. So we ask you this morning to turn in your Bibles to the 9th chapter of St. John, beginning with the 22nd verse of that chapter. There is a Word from the Lord this morning.

I was happy to see our dear sister here today. She knows when she comes home, we're just so happy to see her. You can look at her and tell that she's doing well. I wish she had testified today, because she always has a powerful testimony. You might look at her and say, "Oh, she so quiet," but if you missed Sunday school this morning, she said that when she was on the bus, the driver said to her, "Thank you for the sermon." So that lets me know right there, a lot of times we don't think we're saying very much, but if we just open our mouths and let the Lord use us, God said His Word will go out and not come back void. It will accomplish all those things which God intended for it to accomplish. So I'm mindful this morning, it's not just that I have to stand behind the pulpit to preach. Everywhere I go, I'm preaching and telling people about Jesus.

Let us open the service this morning with "Amazing Grace, how sweet the sound that saved a wretch like me. I once was lost, but now I'm found, was blind, but now I see."

Oh, gracious Father, we come this morning asking You, heavenly Father, if You would use these lips of clay. Oh, heavenly Father, not my will, but Thy will be done. Oh, heavenly Father, we pray now, that as I would lift You up, God, that You would get the glory. We praise You today, that we can stand upon Your Word; for heaven and earth will pass away, but Your Word will stand forever. Thank You, Lord God, for the Spirit that's in this place right now.

Thank You, Lord God, that we can lift you up, magnify and glorify Your wonderful name. Thank You, Jesus, for what You're doing today, in a mighty way. Lord, we're not begging You today: we're calling and asking in Your name, for there's power in Your name. There's healing in Your wonderful name, Lord God, and we praise You for that today. Thank You, Father, for what You're doing right now. Oh, heavenly Father, we praise You right now, for the victory that is not in man, it is not in us, but the victory is in Jesus Christ, for what You did on the cross. We praise You today that we have the joy that the world didn't give, and the world can't take away. We have a peace that passes all understanding. Now, Lord, I've been to the potter's house, and while I was there, You gave me a message. We praise You now, for what You're doing and going to do, in Jesus' name. Thank God, thank God, thank God.

Somebody would say this morning, "Is there a Word from the Lord?" There's always a Word from the Lord. It may not come the way the you feel it should come, it may not come in the way you think it ought to come, but there's always a Word from God.

In St. John, the 9th chapter this morning, beginning at the 22nd verse:

> 22. These words spake his parents, because they feared the Jews: for the Jews had agreed already, that if any man did confess that he was Christ, he should be put out of the synagogue.
> 23. Therefore said his parents, He is of age; ask him.
> 24. Then again called they the man that was blind, and said unto him, Give God the praise: we know that this man is a sinner.
> 25. He answered and said, Whether he be a sinner or no, I know not: one thing I know, that, whereas I was blind, now I see.
> 26. Then said they to him again, What did he to thee? how opened he thine eyes?
> 27. He answered them, I have told you already, and ye did not hear: wherefore would ye hear it again? will ye also be his disciples?
> 28. Then they reviled him, and said, Thou art his disciple; but we are Moses' disciples.
> 29. We know that God spake unto Moses: as for this fellow, we know not from whence he is.

30. The man answered and said unto them, Why herein is a marvellous thing, that ye know not from whence he is, and yet he hath opened mine eyes.

31. Now we know that God heareth not sinners: but if any man be a worshipper of God, and doeth his will, him he heareth.

I want to talk today from that 27th verse this morning, "A Daring Testimony." Would you say that with me? A Daring Testimony. Verse 27 reads, again:

"He answered them, I have told you already, and ye did not hear: wherefore would ye hear it again? will ye also be his disciples?"

Many of us have a testimony, and our testimonies are different. They come in different ways. They come in different forms, and they come in different fashions. Mother Watkins gave her daring testimony this morning, when she was talking about what the Lord has done for her, and one thing about God, He is still dealing with us, every second of the day.

We see in the Scripture this morning, a man born blind, a man that was a sinner, according to the tradition of that day. The man's testimony was, "I was blind and I could not see." Verse 26, "Then said they to him again, What did he to thee? how opened he thine eyes?" Here, this morning, we can see that there are many today who need their eyes opened. Only Jesus can give you a testimony this morning. I'm grateful to God today that each one of us has a testimony, a testimony of the day or the hour that Christ came into our lives. Maybe He came into your life on a Monday. Maybe He came into your life on a Tuesday. Maybe it was on a Wednesday, Thursday, Friday. Maybe it was on a Saturday or Sunday, but each one of us has a testimony of what God has done for us.

There were two unusual men living in Jerusalem during the time of Christ. One has come down through history nameless, but we usually refer to him as 'the man born blind.' The whole city was acquainted with him as a beggar. The other man was a rich man of Jerusalem who yearned for Jesus' body at His death, and he buried it in his tomb. In the Gospel of John, there's much more space given to this blind beggar than to any other character. One of the reasons so much space has been given to this blind man is because he took a stand for Christ. Do you know that each of us here this morning has to take a stand for Christ at some time or another? You took a stand when you walked out of your door this morning. You took a stand when you walked into this building. You walked in here, not for the glamour, not for who comes and goes, but you took a stand when you said, "I'm going to the house of the Lord. I'm going to go and lift up His holy name."

Before we begin reading in the ninth chapter of the Gospel of John, we find in the previous chapters where Jesus had been telling the people that He is the Light of the world, and He said if any man should follow after Him, he should not walk in darkness. As we read our Bibles, we quickly find that anywhere Jesus made a statement, He performed a miracle as evidence of the truth concerning that statement. We said on Tuesday night, while we were here at the church building for Bible Studies, that Jesus never takes away something bad and puts something bad in its place. He always puts something good in its place.

Many people I know say to me they are just one drink away from being an alcoholic. But when you have been delivered by the power of God, when you have been delivered by Jesus, He sets you free, and He sets you free indeed. I'm not one drink or one step away from being a sinner, for I'm kept by the power of God. I'm kept by Him and His blood that He shed on the cross. But many of us will say today, "Oh, the devil has been chasing me all day long." Let me tell you why he's chasing you. Because you have something that he wants, and you won't let go of it. I told the sisters that in the revival on Thursday night, and they were shocked at what I said.

I guess this is why I am somewhat disturbed about different denominations. When preachers and teachers start preaching a denomination, they're setting themselves up for a big fall. The Baptist Church can't save you; the Methodist Church, the Catholic Church, the Church of the Living God: no denomination can save you. Only Jesus can save you. Only Jesus can keep you. When you start telling people that, they say that you're too honest. When you start telling people that, they want to stay away from you. As I was fishing this week, I said to some of the brothers, "One thing about the Lord, when you start being honest, people don't want to hear that, because the world says you've got to be dishonest." The world says you've got to backbite, because others backbite. The world says you've got to lie, because others lie. The world says you've got to take, because others take, and you've got to cheat, because others cheat. But Jesus said, "You've got to love your enemies. You've got to love the ones who persecute you. You've got to love the ones who talk about you. You've got to love the ones who slander your name." Society doesn't understand that.

I'm grateful to God this morning. The Bible says, "how can you say you love God whom you've never seen, and you don't love your sisters and your brothers?" He said that you're a liar, and a liar will never enter the kingdom of God. I'm glad this morning, I have the Lord on my side. I'm glad this morning, I have a daring testimony. As I was moving some boxes around this week, I happened to see the sign that was lying on our front yard just a year or so ago, a sign that someone had put the letters 'KKK,' engraved in white on this sign. I'm glad this morning, for the testimonies today. Let me tell you this morning, I must be on somebody's case. I must be making somebody mad by telling them that nobody can do you like Jesus.

I'm glad this morning that I have a testimony, a testimony to let the world know today that Jesus is still alive. He's still alive, giving sight to the blind. Much like this man in the Scripture, in the 9th chapter of St. John, if he testified anything other than the church that they were in, they would put him out of the synagogue.

They can put me out, but I can tell the world today that Jesus lives. They can put me out of the Baptist denomination, but I can tell the world today that Jesus is all you need. I told somebody this week, they could put me out of Everlasting, but I've got to tell somebody that I know my Redeemer. He lives. He lives today, not just on the outside, but down on the inside. You ought to have a daring testimony, so even if they put you out, you can tell ones that Jesus is alive. If they put you in jail, you ought to tell somebody, "My God is able to deliver me." If you put me in the fiery furnace, I know my God is able this morning. I've got a testimony everywhere I go, that Jesus is in control. I'm glad this morning! I run into hundreds of people all week long, and every time I run into them I tell them that with Jesus, the mighty Lamb of God, you don't need what the world has, but put Christ on the inside, and He will make a way out of no way.

Let me testify here this morning, talking about a daring testimony. I had a man tell me, "Let me tell you, Reverend, I can't believe all that you're saying. I can't believe what you're saying sometimes." I told him, "One thing about when you begin to tell the truth, people don't want to hear the truth. They'd rather hear a lie than the truth of God."

You ought to have a testimony everywhere you go. You should be able to say, "I know Jesus is in control." My God is able, and He's big enough to do all things. I'm glad this morning, I can lift up His holy name. I feel it now, the power of God. Let me tell you today, you don't have to pump up the Lord. You shouldn't have to tarry all night long. You ought to have Jesus down the inside. You ought to have Jesus all over you. He ought to walk with you. He ought to tell you that you belong to Him, and you ought to know you've been bought with a price. I'm glad this morning for the evidence of the truth. The man said, "He said He was the Light of the world, and He proved it by giving light to those were both spiritually and physically blind."

Jesus said He is the Resurrection and the Life. He said the evidence was in His Word at the grave of His friend, Lazarus. Let me tell you this morning, if Jesus had said to all the dead at that grave to get up, I believe all the ones that had died would have gotten up from the grave. You ought to have a testimony burning on the inside. I'm glad this morning that Jesus is in control of every situation. This man was born blind, and we find Jesus' disciples asking Him who did the sinning. Jesus told them that neither was it the man nor his parents. It was the condition of the man that gave an opportunity for God to restore sight, by God's power to heal without medicine. I'm glad today, that God is still healing. Oh, bless His name. He's got more medicine in the hem of His garment than any drugstore in the land.

I'm glad today. I needed a healing one day in my own body, and let me tell you what happened. I came to Everlasting on a Sunday morning. I came to the church, and I told the devil, "I'm tired of you. I'm not going to let you cheat me." Let me tell you today, I sat right in one of those chairs, and I asked only the ones who believed in the power of prayer to come. I said, "I want you to lay hands on me because the doctors have done all they can do. Now Doctor Jesus will have to come on in right now." He came in. He healed my body. He came in, and He healed my mind. Do you know Him today, as a Doctor in a sickroom? Let me move on here today.

Many people are kept from Christ. Christ told the beggar to go down to the pool, and He told him to go and wash. No two people are converted at the same time. So many die in their sin, because they spend a lifetime waiting for the conversion of someone else, like a mother, father, friend, or relative. Christ comes in the manner in which you need Him. Let me say that again. Christ comes in the manner in which you need Him, not in a way that you want Him. When you need Him the most, He'll come right on in. Maybe not at the time you think He should come, but I want to tell you this morning, He's never late. He's never early, but He's always right on time. Oh, thank You, Lord, for what You're doing right now.

After a man is converted, while there are spectators who want to give their versions on their religion, when you accept the Lord, something should happen. Something should change. On the inside, there should be a transformation. I'm glad this morning. I've got the Lord all over the inside of me. One writer said, "It's just like fire shut up in my bones."

The apostle Paul said he was the chief of sinners. He told of his conversion everywhere. Everywhere he went, he told somebody about the Damascus road, when Jesus knocked him off his beast and a voice from heaven said, "Saul, Saul, why do you persecute me?" Then Jesus said, "I know you, Saul." He knows every one of us. He's got our address. Oh, bless His name. He's got every hair numbered on our head. It's predestined already what's going to happen. I'm glad today, man doesn't hold your future or my future in his hands, but God holds it all by Himself. The One who sits high and looks low has all power in His hands. He's not just a little god, He's a big God. He's got the whole world in His hands. The Sunday school kids today sang, "He's got the mamas and the papas in His hand, He's got the whole world in His hands." I'm glad today! My hope and trust is in Jesus. I'm glad today; it's not in anything else.

As I move on here this morning, these Pharisees went to the parents of this man so they could give a reason to take the credit away from Jesus. The devil will always try to take from God. But let me tell you, my God is big enough. My God is powerful enough. Oh, glory to His name. He's got more power and more medicine and more healing than any drugstore in the land. But the devil will always try. The Word says, they went to the parents, trying to take away the testimony of what Jesus had done. The man's conversion caused his parents to forsake him. He remained with Jesus when all others had forsaken him. Jesus accepts faith as being sufficient discipleship.

You ought to have a sufficient discipleship. You ought to have a testimony. I'm glad this morning, I've got a testimony, and I'm going to move on here. I've got a testimony that nobody can do me like Jesus. Nobody can do me like the Lord. Oh, bless His name today. I can talk about that wonderful name, the name of Jesus. He woke me up this morning. He started me on my way. I'm glad this morning, I've got a testimony today! Oh, bless His name! Jesus, the mighty Lamb of God, Jesus, my way-maker, Jesus, my All in all! Let me tell you today, put your hands in God's hands. He will make everything all right.

Look at Him hanging there on that cross, blood running down from His hands and His feet. He didn't say a mumbling word, but, "Father, forgive them, for they know not what they do." They stretched Him wide, they pierced Him in His side, blood and water running together, blood running down from His hands and His feet. They put a crown of thorns on His head. He had to die for you and me. They took Him off that cross. They laid Him in a cold, dark tomb. He lay there all day Saturday. He lay there for me, so I could give a testimony. For you, He lay there.

When they try to slander you, don't you worry. When they try to kill you, don't you worry. When they try to do all sorts of evil to you, don't you worry. My God has got all power in His hands.

I'm glad this morning, that He got up! He got up on Sunday morning, with all power in His hands. Let me tell you this morning, it's something about Jesus. He got up as King of kings and Lord of lords! He got up! Buddha is still in the grave. Abraham Lincoln is still in the grave. Martin Luther King is still in the grave. Presidents are still in the grave. Mohammed is still in the grave. But my Jesus got up with all power in His hands! I'm glad this morning that I've got a testimony, that my Jesus lives today. He went all the way back to heaven. When He went back, He sent Something to give me a testimony. He sent me Something that would make me live right. He sent me Something that would make me walk right. He sent me Something down on the inside, when it seems like I'm all on my own. He will take you all the way. I'm glad this morning that Jesus went all the way back to glory. But He sent the Holy Ghost to comfort us.

As I close this morning, let me close with this. I'm glad this morning that Jesus is the Light of the world, and I have a testimony, not from the world, but from the Lord. One day, the story goes, Grace and Mercy were walking along and they had a conversation. Grace told Mercy, "I'm going to meet you in three days. I want to get together with you where we can talk." They were walking along and Grace went one way and Mercy went the other. Let me tell you about God's grace. It's real. It's real! As they were walking in separate directions, three days later they were to meet. Grace was waiting on Mercy, Mercy was late getting there. Grace saw him walking down the road and he knew it was his friend, Mercy.

Mercy came up to him and Grace said, "Look at you man, look your clothes. Looks like you've been in a fire. Look at your hair, it's all over your head. You've got blood stains all over your body."

Mercy said, "I left here a few days ago, and on my way here, I passed by and I heard three boys" — and this is a testimony today of what God is able to do, — "and they were saying, 'our God can deliver us regardless of what we do. We know our God is able today. If we are destroyed, our God is able, and we're going to go and be thrown in the fire, in the fiery furnace.' "

And Mercy said, "I went in to see about the boys, and when I went in, I was there with them all the time."

If you've got a testimony this morning, I don't care what you're going through, you're going to go through it smelling like roses. I've got a picture in my mind that those three boys didn't smell like smoke. They said Jesus was in the midst of them. He not only took the fire out, and the smell, but He took the sting and everything out of it.

Mercy said, "This is why my clothes are looking like they're looking, because those boys cried for mercy."

And Mercy said, "I knew I was going to be late, and I heard a man who was on his knees. He was praying. He was talking with his God and I happened to listen to what the man was saying."

This is testimony time. That man was Daniel, in the lions' den. He heard the man talk with God. You ought to be able to talk with God. You ought to be able to call on His name, morning, noon, and night. And Daniel called on the Lord.

Mercy said, "I went in and I held the lions' jaws all night while brother Daniel slept on a lion. This is why my coat is torn in some places."

And Mercy said, "I knew I was going to be late but I made my way. As I made my way I saw a group of people, and they were hanging a man on the cross. They were hanging a man between two thieves, one on the right, and one on the left. I heard them say, 'He's the King of the Jews.' I heard Him call. When they nailed His hands to the cross I went all the way up there and I took the sting out of the cross."

And then Grace said, "And then I led Him all the way home."

You ought to have a daring testimony this morning, that nobody can do you like the Lord. Nobody can do you like Jesus. I thank the Lord this morning, God is totally in control. We ought to have a testimony that nobody can do us like the Lord.

You can come to Jesus today. You can have a daring testimony. Come to Jesus.

The Extension of the Christian Church
Matthew 16:13-18

Let us pray.

Our Father and our God, we thank You now for this day. Thank You, heavenly Father, for the Word You've given us. Oh, heavenly Father, we pray now that You would use me, Thy minister, in a mighty way. Oh, heavenly Father, not my will, but Thy will be done. Oh, heavenly Father, give us a Word from the Lord today. Oh, heavenly Father, we pray now that You would open up our eyes today. Open up our ears today, that we may not just be a hearer, but a doer of Your Word. Thank You, Lord God, for this place of worship. Thank You, oh, heavenly Father. Where there's much prayer, there's much power. Where there's little prayer, there's little power. Where there's no prayer, there's no power. We're believing today, Lord God, that much prayer has brought us to this appointed time, and this appointed place. Oh, heavenly Father, we thank You right now, for what You've done. We thank You, Lord God, for what You're going to do. Now, Lord, bless us in a mighty way. Use me in a mighty way. Use these lips of clay, that I might testify and witness for You, the risen Christ, the One who has all power in Your hands. What a Friend You are today! A Friend to the motherless, a Friend to the ones that are without today. Thank You, Jesus, for what You are going to do. In Jesus' name we pray, amen, amen and amen.

Would you turn in your Bibles with me to the book of St. Matthew, the 16th chapter? The question is asked today, "Is there a Word from the Lord?" We know there is always a Word from God, amen? Praise God. Turn to Matthew, the 16th chapter, verse 13 this morning.

13. When Jesus came into the coasts of Caesarea Philippi, he asked his disciples, saying, Whom do men say that I the Son of man am?
14. And they said, Some say that thou art John the Baptist: some, Elias; and others, Jeremias, or one of the prophets.
15. He saith unto them, But whom say ye that I am?
16. And Simon Peter answered and said, Thou art the Christ, the Son of the living God.

17. And Jesus answered and said unto him, Blessed art thou, Simon Barjona: for flesh and blood hath not revealed it unto thee, but my Father which is in heaven.
18. And I say also unto thee, That thou art Peter, and upon this rock I will build my church; and the gates of hell shall not prevail against it.

I was asked the other day if I thought church people were fulfilling what Jesus said we must do. I answered, "Yes and no." But I also said, "God's Word must stand." Jesus spoke it and said, "Upon this rock I build my church, and the gates of hell cannot prevail against it." Jesus went on to say that the devil would come against the church, but he would not be able to overtake it, because of the foundation. I want to preach to you, from the thought of the subject this morning, "The Extension of the Christian Church." Would you say that with me? "The Extension of the Christian Church."

The most important influence in the world today is the Christian church. Let nobody tell you this morning that the church of Jesus Christ is failing. Let nobody tell you this morning that no one's getting saved, and that everyone who's confessing to be a Christian today is on their way to hell. Let nobody tell you that this morning. Let nobody tell you that all of the Catholics, all of the Methodists, all of the Episcopalians, or all of the other denominations are on their way to hell. Let nobody tell you that today, because that's not true. That's a lie. The devil is a liar.

Whatever denomination it is, you've got some people who are calling upon the name of the Lord, the extension of the Christian church. This is, of course, because it is dedicated and directed to the course and cause of salvation, which is to be accomplished through common means and common men. It is heaven's way of getting salvation into the midst of the human family. Every one of us who has unsaved loved ones should not be praying that God would give them more material substance. We should not be praying that God would heal their bodies and give them longevity. We should not be praying that God would give them more prosperity. But we ought to be praying, as the Christian church, that God would save them, that God would give them salvation, which is free to every one who asks for it. I feel like preaching this morning. Praise God!

I preach like this every time that I get a chance, because it may be my last time. Someone said a week or so ago, "We would join

Everlasting, but the preacher talks about Jesus too much. So, therefore, we won't join there, because all he talks about is Jesus." But let me tell you this morning, nobody can do you like Jesus! Nobody can do you like the Lord! Nobody can do you like Jesus, who gave His life, that we might have life, and life more abundantly.

When Jesus was bringing His earthly ministry to a conclusion, while talking to His disciples one day, He made mention of the church and its future program in the world. When Jesus came into the coast of Caesarea Philippi, He asked His disciples, "Whom do men say that I am?" And some said, "Thou art Elias." Some said, "Thou art John the Baptist." Some said, "Thou art Jeremias, or one of the other prophets." But Jesus said, "But whom do you say that I am?" And Peter said, "Thou art the Christ, the Son of the living God."

I want to ask you this morning, whom do you say Jesus is? Is He Mary's Baby, the One that was born in Bethlehem? Is He the King of kings and Lord of lords? John, on the Isle of Patmos, said, "I saw Him on the Lord's day." One of the other prophets said, "I saw Him as a Wheel in the middle of a wheel." One of the other prophets said, "I saw Him when my mother died." Isaiah said he saw Him when King Uzziah died, and he saw Him high and lifted up, and His train filled the temple. But I want to ask you this morning, whom do you say Jesus is? I want to testify this morning and say, He's my All in all. He's all that I need to stand and tell a dying world that the wages of sin is death, but the gift of God is eternal life. He's all that you need, as you walk around town. He's all that you need, when they ask you, "What happened to you a few weeks ago?" You can tell somebody, "I once was lost, but now am found! I once was blind, but now I see!"

I'm glad this morning, Brother Paul, everywhere he went, he talked about his conversion on the Damascus road. I don't know about you this morning, but you ought to have a testimony, and every where you go, you ought to let it shine. Every where you go, you ought to tell somebody, "I know the Lord will make a way for you! I know the Lord will be a burden bearer for you! I know the Lord can heal your body, because what He's done for me, He'll do the same for you!" I feel It now, moving down on the inside!

But whom do you say the Son of man is? Oh, bless His name today! And Jesus answered and said unto him, "Blessed art thou, Simon Bar-jona, for flesh and blood hath not revealed it unto you, but my Father, my Father, which is in heaven!" I want to ask you this morning, do you have a Father who will be a Lawyer for you? Do you have a Father who will be a Doctor for you? Do you have a Father who will provide for your every need? I'm glad this morning! My heavenly Father is above! My earthly father died about a year ago, but he gave me something! Thank you, Dad, for what you gave me! You gave me a faith so that I can go on, in the Lord! If you never see me again on this earth, I pray that I've given you a faith that you will stand on the Word of God! Thank You, Jesus! Whom do you say that the Son of Man is?

Jesus answered him and said, "Upon this rock I will build my church, and the gates of hell shall not prevail against it." Somebody would say this morning that the foundation was built on Peter. Oh, no, it wasn't! It was built on what Peter said: "You are the Son of God." Whom do you say that Jesus is this morning? Is He, this morning, your All in all? Are you an extension of the church of Jesus Christ? Everywhere you go, are you letting your light shine? Everywhere you go, are you telling somebody, "I know the Lord! I love Him this morning! I know the Lord will make a way for you!" Oh, let me tell you this morning, it's not that the devil is not gonna be after you, because he will, but you can tell Satan, "Can't nobody do me like Jesus! Nobody can do me like the Lord!" Nobody, this morning! He can heal your mind! I say to you, stand on the Word! The Word of God! I'm glad this morning! I know Jesus will make a way for you! I know Jesus will! Oh, bless His name today!

In this declaration, Jesus was setting forth His purpose for the future, for He said, "I will build my church." "I will build my church," a projected vision for ages to come. Here we are, 2000 years later, and we're still talking about Jesus, the mighty Lamb of God. Somebody was saying they serve a little, bitty god. But my God is a big God! All power! All power! All power is in His hands! Holy Ghost power! Wonder-working power! I feel It now, moving, the Holy Ghost, moving down on the inside! When He said, "Upon this rock," He refers us to depth of truth wrapped up in the declaration of the statement of Peter, when Peter said, "Thou art the Christ, the Son of the living God." I love that about the Lord! My God is not dead! He's alive! He's alive! Oh, bless His name today! He's alive! I'm glad about that!

'To build' means to construct. It means to enlarge and to stretch forth the strides of life extending to the thoughts of men. I'm glad this morning, I've got a foundation — oh, bless His name today! —

and it's not on the Baptist Church! I've got a foundation and it's built on the Rock, the Rock of Jesus, my All in all!

I heard a story just a few months ago. A man had some property, and he had to clear the land. He had all these trees, and some of these trees were over a hundred years old. And the man got a crew to come out and excavate the land, and find out what needed to be done. They cut down all the trees, all except one tree. The man said to the team, "I want you to take this tree out." They went up and looked at this tree, and it was really tall. It must've been sixty feet tall. They began to cut it down. They cut it down, all the way to the roots. Then they got another contractor and he said, "We want you to go down and dig up the roots, so we can plow the land and build on it." The crew dug deep, and the more they dug, the deeper the roots were. The roots were as deep as the tree was tall. The roots were just that deep. I'm glad this morning! You ought to have roots! I don't care how tall you are! You ought to be rooted upon the Word of God! You ought to be rooted in Jesus! And the story goes, they dug deeper and deeper, and deeper and deeper! And when they got all the way down to where the roots were, all the roots that went down so deep, they were all tangled up, and they were wrapped around a huge rock.

I want to tell you this morning, your foundation ought to be around a Rock, and that Rock ought to be Jesus, the mighty Lamb of God! In speaking of building, Jesus did not mean the physical expansion, but in other ways, more noble. The building program of the church is to be carried through believers, and proportioned to reach and inspire mankind onward and upward to higher heights. Jesus came into the midst of men for the purpose of saving men from themselves, and for their God. Let me say that again today! Jesus came into the midst of men for the purpose of saving men from themselves, and for their God, who made them. So Jesus' plan of salvation is the church. It's not the building that you're in today, but it's the body of Christ, the ones that Jesus said that He gave His life for! I'm glad this morning, for Jesus, because of His mighty moves in men.

The Christian church has worked itself into units in order to reach all men in their various forms, in their habits and ways of life. You might say this morning, "There's a church in Tacoma, there's one in Seattle, there's one in Los Angeles, there's one in Portland, there's one up in the heights, there's one over there." Jesus said, "I give my life." Oh, bless His name today! And He said there are many members, but there's only one Body, and that's the Body of Christ. I'm glad! I carry the church! You carry the church every where you go, down on the inside! Jesus said, "I build my church, not with bricks and mortar, but I build it with people, the people of God!"

Although bricks and mortar are materials used in building the physical structure, the place where the congregation assembles for worship, Jesus said, "My church is not the bricks. It's not the mortar! But My church is the body of believers who have come together in My name!" Standing on the Word! Standing on the promises of Christ, my Savior! "My church" — oh, bless His name — "is in the hearts of men!" I'm glad! I'm glad today! I have it! And the world didn't give it to me! You ought to have it! And the world can't take it away! Somebody said, "This peace that I have, the world didn't give it to me, and the world can't take it away!" I want to tell you this morning, if it comes from the Lord, you ought to keep it! It ought to be gripped around the Rock of Jesus! I'm glad this morning! Jesus said, "I will build my church, and it won't be from bricks, and it won't be from mortar."

One of the greatest troubles with the people of the time of Jesus, as it is today: the need of a change of mind as the demanding cry. Jesus said, "I want to change your mind. I want to fix your mind. I want your mind stayed on Me, not on anything else, but put your mind on Me!" David said, "My mind, and my eyes have I put on the Lord." You ought to have your mind on Him this morning! One of the greatest troubles with people of this day, they've got their minds on everything else. But let me tell you this morning, nobody can do you like the Lord!

Peter said to Jesus, "Thou art the Christ, the Son of the living God." And from this declaration, He moved to set the church in motion. It has been moving on ever since! Let nobody tell you that it's not moving on! The extension of the Christian church is going to move on until Jesus comes back for it. Oh, I'm glad this morning, not only through the mind will the church be extended, but through the character of men. You've got to have character today, that others will see and glorify your Father! Somebody would say this morning, "I can live any kind of way." But let me tell you this morning, you've got to live according to the Word of God. Jesus said, "I'm coming back. I'm not coming to this earth, but I'm coming back for a church, and they're gonna meet me in the air!" I'm glad today!

We're gonna meet Him in the air! Will you be ready when He comes? I'm glad this morning, He's coming back!

The world can't always hear what we say, but they are watching what we do. (Oh, bless His name today!) Your actions ought to speak louder than what you say. If we're going to be an influence, and extend an influence of the church into the world, we must watch and change our patterns of conduct! Oh, bless His name today! Everywhere you go, you ought to say, "Lord, I want You to use me." Everywhere you go, you ought to say, "Jesus, use me today! Jesus, use me on my job! Jesus, use me in the grocery store! Jesus, use me, Lord, in Thy service!"

When thinking about extending the influence of the church, we do not have in mind the physical building, but the people of God! You are the church! Everywhere you go, you carry the church in you! Don't let anybody tell you it's the building that you're in, but the church of God is marching on! The church of God is moving on! It's not dead, like a lot of folks and the devil want you to think! My God is still saving! He's still filling! He's still sanctifying! He's still delivering! He's still raising up bowed-down heads! He's still curing whole bodies today! He's still saving drug addicts and prostitutes, and all kinds of sinners. My God is able today!

On the Friday afternoon following the crucifixion, Jesus went to hell. When He stepped in the door, hell asked Him, "Who are You, and what are You doing here?" Jesus said, "I am Adam, the last Adam. I died on the cross a few hours ago, so I could get down here. I know you only enter hell through the door of death." And Jesus said, "Look at my hands!" Oh, bless His name today! "Look at my feet! I've just come from the cross!" And He said, "Look at my brow, and look at my side." He said, "I suffered all of these embarrassments so I could come down and get the keys to the vault of men's death and punishment."

Let me say to you this morning, you can't save yourself. Jesus is the only One who can save you. You can't draw yourself. Only Jesus, by the Holy Ghost, can draw you. And if He draws you, He'll keep you! Death and hell objected but Jesus persisted and conquered in His mission. Nobody knew this until Sunday, when He arose.

On the Isle of Patmos, when John met Jesus he said, "I met Him, and when I met Him, He made a difference in my life." Let me ask you this morning, has Jesus made a difference in your life? Has Jesus turned your midnights into days? Has Jesus made a difference in your life? I'm glad today!

They hanged Him on that cross, blood running down from His hands and His feet, but He didn't say a mumbling word, but, "Father!" My Father today, who art in heaven! It ought to be something about the will of God! You ought to say, "Your will, Lord; not my will, but Your will, be done on earth" — I feel It now! — "as it is in heaven! Your will, Lord, every way I turn! Your will, Lord, every breath I take! Your will, Lord, every drop of food I put in my mouth. Your will, Lord, every step I take."

I'm glad today, that Jesus was hanging there, on the cross, blood running down from His hands and His feet, but He didn't say a mumbling Word, but, "Father, forgive them, for they know not what they do." Can you tell somebody, "I forgive you today, for what you've done. I forgive you for what you said." I forgive them, Lord! Oh, bless His name today! Don't wait until you get to heaven to begin to love. You've got to love down here. Somebody told me a few months ago, "I'm going to love when I get to heaven." Let me tell you today, you're going to have to start right here! This is the preparation ground, getting ready to make heaven your home!

Look at Jesus! They took Him down off that cross. They placed Him in a cold, dark tomb. But let me tell you — Oh, bless His name today! — He got up! He laid there, but He got up! He laid there all day Saturday, and all night Saturday night! I'm glad this morning, He got up Sunday morning! All power was in His hands! All power! We're going to lay down one day, but we're going to get up with resurrection power! We're going to get up with saving power! I'm glad this morning, He got up! I'm glad! He got on that cloud and he went all the way back to glory! But He sent me Something! He sent you Something that would lead you and guide you. He said, "I'm going to send you the Holy Ghost. It will lead you and guide you. I'm going to send you Something, when they talk about you, It's going to be there with you. When you run out of everything, It's going to be there with you. When you can't see your way, It's going to be there with you. I'm glad today, for the Holy Ghost — oh, glory to God! — only Jesus can send to us. Oh, bless His name today!

Come to Jesus.

I Just Can't Keep It to Myself
Mark 1:40-45

Truly we're thankful to the Lord this morning, for He is our Savior today. I want to ask you if you would turn in your Bibles to St. Mark, the first chapter. The question is asked, "Is there a Word from the Lord?" I want to say there is always a Word from God. It may not come in the way that you think it should come, but there's always a Word from the Lord. Sometimes it comes as a still, quiet voice. Sometimes it comes at midnight. Sometimes it comes by the way of an animal.

This week, I had somewhat of a heartening situation. I had to put my dog to sleep this week. I've always said he was the best four-legged friend that a preacher could have. I loved that dog. He got to the point where he had to be put to sleep, because I could not stand to see him suffer any longer. But I'm mindful today, that God answers prayer. I remember the first part of the year, when he was down in his hips, and he was doing very badly. I began to pray for that dog, and began to pray over his body, and he began to come back. There were many that said, "We thought that dog was dead." But I'm a living witness today that God answers prayer, and not only will He supply our needs, but He'll give us the desires of our hearts. I'm grateful to God that God will give us the desires of our hearts, if we obey Him, if we obey His Word. If we line up with His Word, He will be faithful in what He said He will do.

St. Mark, chapter one, beginning at the 40th verse. There is a story here today. Let us read together, five verses.

40. And there came a leper to him, beseeching him, and kneeling down to him, and saying unto him, If thou wilt, thou canst make me clean.
41. And Jesus, moved with compassion, put forth his hand, and touched him, and saith unto him, I will; be thou clean.
42. And as soon as he had spoken, immediately the leprosy departed from him, and he was cleansed.
43. And he straitly charged him, and forthwith sent him away;
44. And saith unto him, See thou say nothing to any man: but go thy way, shew thyself to the priest, and offer for thy cleansing those things which Moses commanded, for a testimony unto them.

45. But he went out, and began to publish it much, and to blaze abroad the matter, insomuch that Jesus could no more openly enter into the city, but was without in desert places: and they came to him from every quarter.

Let us pray.

Father, we thank You now for what You're going to do today. We praise You, Father, for Your Word. We praise You, oh, heavenly Father, that faith cometh by hearing, and hearing by the Word of God. Thank You, Lord Jesus, that we are about to be used by You. Oh, heavenly Father, not my will, but Thy will be done. You said, Lord God, if I open my mouth, that You would give me words to say. But first of all, Lord God, we need something in us to say. Oh, heavenly Father, we praise You today, that Your Word will go out and not come back void, but It will accomplish those things for which You intend It to accomplish. Oh, heavenly Father, let Your Spirit and Your Word go from beyond these four walls, go out into Clark County, Lord God, wherever sin is raging. Go out, Lord God, wherever ones are complacent. Go out, Lord God, where others have forgotten all about You, and are giving themselves the glory. Lord God, we pray now for the Spirit of God, that It will move and have free course this day, all through this day. In Jesus' name we pray. Thank You, Lord God, for what You've done and are doing and going to do, in Jesus' name. Amen, amen and amen.

I want to talk about, from those few verses that we read this morning, the thought of the subject today, "I just can't keep it to myself." Would you say that with me? I just can't keep it to myself. You might say today, that's rather comical, that topic. But if you noticed from the reading this morning, this man whom we read about, this leper, he just could not keep it to himself. By him not keeping it to himself, he put Jesus in a very delicate situation.

The other day, I told a group that the devil was right there with Jesus in the beginning. I also said that the devil hears everything we say, and He knows everything we do. Do you know that the devil knows the Word of God better than some of us? Why do you think that so many of us are so devastated? Why do you think most of us get mad so quickly? Why do you think so many of us always find ourselves down and out in our spirit? It's not because of God. It's because of the devil. He always wants to twist the Word of God and make it into a lie. But Jesus said, "It is written, Man shall not live by bread alone, but by every Word that proceedeth out of the mouth of

God." We remember the story of Jesus, when He came out of the water, the devil was right there with Him. And the devil tempted Him. And the Word says that Jesus said to the devil, "Get thee behind me, Satan. It is written, Thou shalt not tempt the Lord thy God." I'm mindful this morning that the devil knows. Sisters and brothers, it is not good to tell everybody everything. You ought to keep something to yourself, between you and God. I just can't keep it to myself.

Our text takes us to an encounter between Jesus and a man. The Bible does not bother identifying the man by name, for it is not important that we know what this man's name is. His condition in life is more important than his title. The Gospel writer, Mark, simply says, "then, a leper," not "a man," not "then, a believer," no, that's not specific enough. Not "then, a Hebrew." No, that's not deep enough either. Not even "a traveler." That's not helpful to us, to get us to see what's going on. It says, "then, a leper," which meant that his body was covered with leprosy. It paints to us a picture of what's going on, for it says, "then, a leper." This man was special, for he raised up to us an examination in the Scriptures. For it says, "then, a leper," which meant God was going to do a work in his life: and this is what God is trying to do in the world today. Then, a backbiter. Then, a sinner. Then, a murderer. Then, a homosexual. Right on down the list. But then they were. But when they come to Jesus, that's all passed away. This man was special, for it says, "then, a leper." He is brought from the depths of humanity to the permanent record of the Scriptures. For it says, "then, a leper." The subject, again, this morning, "I just can't keep it to myself."

The spotlight shines on him who has never seen the light. In other words, the man wasn't saved. He didn't know or have a relationship with Jesus Christ. But yet and still, then, a leper. Then, the Scripture says, a leper came to Him. The leper came to Jesus for various reasons. Primarily, this leper must've heard of the great works of healings and miracles that Jesus had done. If you had leprosy, nobody wanted to be around you, because, at that time, there was no cure for leprosy.

I'm mindful of a man by the name of Naaman. This man was a leper. He wasn't born a leper, but he had acquired leprosy. The Scripture says, in the Old Testament, when Naaman had acquired leprosy, his friends began to become few. Even his own family began to put him off by himself. Something about us, as Christians, as children of God, we don't have many friends.

A few years ago, I had a nickname. Some called me, at that time, the Wizard. They would say, "Here comes Willie the Wizard," because they knew I always had something going on. But let me tell you this morning, then, a wizard, but now, a child of God. It's something about God. When He comes into your life, He turns your midnights into days. Oh, I feel like preaching this morning.

Oh, let me tell you today, as the Scriptures have said, that Naaman was a leper, and he began to really get sick with sores all over his body. Naaman's wife heard one of the slave girls in their home talk about a man who had cured people of leprosy. Then the slave girl was telling Mrs. Naaman about the leprosy that she saw the man of God heal. And the story goes on to say that when Mrs. Naaman went to her husband, she told him about a man who cured people of leprosy. And then Mr. Naaman said to Mrs. Naaman, "How many did you say that the slave girl said had been healed of leprosy?" (Let me tell you this morning that there ought to be certain things that you keep to yourself. You ought not tell anybody.) And the Scripture says that the man Naaman sent a word by the slave girl, to tell this man of God that he wanted to see him, and he wanted him to heal him of leprosy. And the story goes, the man of God didn't go to see what Naaman had, but he sent a word to Naaman. He said, "Tell brother Naaman to go down to the river and wash seven times."

There's something about being obedient to the man of God. The reason many people aren't being blessed is because they don't want to listen to the man of God. You ought to be able to listen, and get a Word from the Lord. You ought to be obedient to somebody. I'm mindful this morning of the many weddings I've done. Many young wives or wives-to-be will say, "I don't want 'obedient' in my marriage vows. I don't want to be obedient to anybody. I don't want to be obedient to any man." But let me tell you this morning, when they begin to feel that way, their marriage is already going down the tubes. You ought to be obedient to somebody.

The man of God told Naaman, "Go down and wash seven times." It says that Brother Naaman went down to the river there and began to wash. When he washed one time, nothing happened. He washed the second time, and nothing happened. He washed the third time and nothing happened. He washed the forth time and nothing happened. Let me tell you this morning, it's something about being faithful to the Word of God. You may get discouraged, but you ought to not give up. You may feel doubt, but you ought to not let it do anything to what the Lord has given you. You ought to know today, whatever discouragement you're going through, you ought to keep it to yourself. I'm glad this morning for the story today. Oh, bless God's holy name! And the story says that Naaman washed the fifth time, and nothing happened. He washed the sixth time and nothing happened. Oh, bless God! The seventh time, he went down into the water, and the seventh time, he came up, and he looked at his hands. His hands looked new. He looked at his feet, and they were, too! I'm glad this morning! God is still healing! I'm glad this morning, God is still moving in a mighty way.

But let me move on here today. From the outside, that would appear appropriate, the leper came to Jesus seeking healing. Isn't that wonderful, he came to the Lord and he asked for a healing? He came to Jesus just as he was. If you're willing today, if you come to Jesus, you can be made clean. I want to tell you this morning, whatever it is, you can be made whole, not just in your body, but in your mind. I'm glad this morning, God's will must be done.

Lepers were social outcasts, cut off from the realm of society. For many years, this leper was one of those on the outside looking in. He wanted his life back. He wanted to be part of the crowd. The Word says, "Jesus, moved with compassion." Jesus genuinely empathizes and feels what we're going through. Let nobody tell you this morning that the Lord doesn't know. He knows all about it. He knows what's going on in the world and in you today. He knows — oh, bless His name today! — God knows what's going on. I'm glad that He had compassion on this leper.

As I move on here, our trust today would be stronger if we learned how to go to God with our problems. I'm glad this morning, I can go to God. I'm not saying I don't need anybody, but I ought to be able to go to God and tell Him all about my trials, all about my tribulations, all about the joy that I need. I wish, today, that others were here, to hear what the Lord has to say. But God is in control of that, too.

I'm a firm believer that I'm not God — oh, bless His name! — and I don't hold any answers to any of your problems. I can show you to God. We go to the courts. We go to the committees. We go to the board, trying to move things in the church. But I want to say today, if you want to move things in the church, you've got to go to the One who runs the church. You've got to go to the One, to God in prayer, to tell the Lord all about what you want Him to do.

I just can't keep it to myself. I'm glad, today, for the mighty Lamb of God. The leper was cleansed. This was the height of Jesus'

66

work in the chapter of Mark. This leper was raised up as a shining example of Jesus' ministry in this particular chapter. He healed many folk, but no one was raised up like this man. I'm glad that God is still raising up! He's still pouring out His Spirit.

I heard someone say the other day that the church is dying and all of God's churches are on their way to hell. Let me tell you today, that's a trick of the devil! God's church is marching on! Not the church building, but the children of God. There are still some people who are praying today. There are still some people who are on their knees, before the Lord, and talking with God.

I just can't keep it to myself this morning. But the paradox is that this man was also a problem. He was a problem to the ministry of Jesus. Jesus told him, "See to it that you say nothing to anyone. But go your way, show yourself to the priests, and offer for your cleansing those things which Moses commanded, as a testimony to them," which meant he was supposed to give the church some of his material. Give them a piece of money to glorify God. This leper was not only cleansed, but he was disobedient.

Let me tell you this morning, we've got a lot of disobedient people that have been in the church for a long time. They're disobedient to what the preacher has to say. They're disobedient to the commandments of God's Word. They're disobedient to the covenant that's on the wall. But I'm glad this morning. He did not do what the Lord wanted him to do. He did, rather, what he wanted to do. You've got ones in the church today, as long as they are glorified, they are all right. But when you don't glorify them, or pat them on the back, you've got hell on every hand. I'm glad for Everlasting today. As I walk in and out of these doors, I'm glad I don't have a board to tell me, "You can't preach like that." I'm glad I don't have a committee to tell me, "You can't change the carpet." I'm glad we don't have somebody to tell me, "You can't give anybody a bus ticket to ride the bus, to try to get a job."

I'm glad this morning. I'm glad today. I've got free course in the ministry of God, and everywhere I go, I want to be able to tell somebody, "I know the Lord, He has been good." I've been in this county almost twenty years, oh, bless God's name! I'm the most free this year, more than I've ever been. I'm getting more free every day, more free in the Spirit to praise His name, more free in the Spirit to lift up His holy name! I'm glad this morning! I can go on with the Lord! Oh, help me today, Jesus, to preach Your Word! I'm glad today! I just can't keep it to myself! I love the Lord today! I feel it coming on! It's moving, down on the inside of me. I feel the Wheel turning, in the middle of me right now! Oh, thank the Lord! Oh, bless His name today!

I don't have time to explore the theological interpretations of the text. I don't have time to deal with the post-resurrection and the matter of whether the leper was saved or not. I don't know. All I can say today, he was disobedient to Jesus. And let me tell you today, justice will prevail. I'm glad. I can't keep it to myself. I'm trying to hurry here. What is it, I can't keep? Oh, bless His name today!

But let me say, this leper was disobedient. He spent his time doing other than what Jesus had commanded. We've got churches that are filled all over this world with people that are not doing what God commanded. They're doing what the denomination would have them to do. I've got a dear brother, he's been pastoring for over 15 years. Every Sunday, they have a layout of what he's supposed to preach. Four Sundays on tithes, four Sundays on the blood, four Sundays on salvation. But I can preach the Word everywhere I go.

Sometimes it's best to keep the blessings of God all to yourself. A lack of humility is killing the church of God right now. Not everybody wants to lift up the Lord, but they want to glorify themselves. This leper wasn't glorifying God, he was glorifying himself. "Look at me, look what I've got now. I've got my body healed. I've got my family back. I've got my job back. I've got everything back." But when you glorify God, you're not concerned about what you've got. All you know, as the other man was healed, we talked about just a few Sundays ago, he said, "I don't know who He was, I don't know where He's from. I just know I was blind, and I could not see. He touched my eyes, and He made me whole." I'm glad today! I've got a testimony this morning. I just can't keep it to myself today!

Sometimes it's better to keep the blessings of God to yourself. We come to church bragging on our degrees. We brag on our own righteousness. We brag on our own position of authority. We brag on who we are. We brag on when we knew them, and how much we've known them. I'm glad this morning. When you come to the house of God, you ought to come worshipping the name of the Lord. You ought to come knowing, "I didn't come to gossip, I didn't come to lie. I came to worship the Lord in Spirit and in truth. I came to magnify His name." I don't know what you came to do, but I came to lift Him up. It's a terrible thing to brag about yourself. Bragging often will lead to state of false euphoria. Some people get high off cocaine. Some people get high off alcohol. And then some people get high off bragging about themselves.

But I say, it's dangerous when you brag. There ought to be something you keep to yourself. Because of this leper, the ministry of Jesus was changed in this area of Galilee. If only he would have kept quiet. But the problem was not his mouth. It was his heart. Everywhere he went, he was telling them, "There's a man named Jesus. I was a leper, and he raised me up. Look at me now." He was not like Paul. Paul, too, was sick, and God healed him. Paul, too, was a sinner, and God saved him. But everything he did, he was glorifying God. Not me, Jesus, but You do the work in my life. I'm glad this morning. If this leper only would have been obedient, and had an obedient heart. You know, our churches would be better places if we had some obedient hearts, obedient to the Word of God, obedient to what thus saith the Lord.

I'm glad, I'm so glad today, that I can listen. I don't have to always be running my mouth, but I can listen to the Spirit of God. We want to come to the Lord's house and pick and choose our own seats. We want to get mad if our name is left off the program. We want to get mad if folks don't call our names like they should. When Jesus tells us to do something, we do the exact opposite thing. When God tells us to witness, we begin to gossip. When God says 'go,' we stop. When God says 'tithe,' we tip. When God says 'preach,' we sleep. When God says 'build,' we tear down. When God says 'arrive,' we stay home. When God says 'help,' we hurt. When God says 'go forward,' we hunt for reverse.

The leper told everything that happened. I'm reminded today of a man who witnessed a car accident. Three folks got killed in the accident. The man was asked by the police, "Did you see it?" He said, "No, I didn't." A few days later, the television station said there was a $10,000 reward for anyone who saw the accident. Suddenly the man appeared and said, "I saw everything that happened." The police officer asked, "Why didn't you tell us that, at the scene of the accident?" The man said, "You weren't offering $10,000." The Lord wants us to do the right thing, not for a reward here on earth, but because it's the right thing to do.

And what Jesus offered to this leper, he's offering to each of us. He wants us to do the work of the Lord. He wants us to follow the Word of God. If you follow His Word today, His ministry will go forward. If you follow His Word today, the devil will tremble — oh, bless His name today! I'm a witness this morning, if we that are here today would get on one accord, we will see the devil be bound in a mighty way! I say to you today, get your mind on the Lord. Get your heart fixed on Jesus.

I'm glad this morning, as I move on here, I just can't keep it to myself. This leper had talked so much, Jesus could not go where the sinners were. That's what happens today. We cut off folks from Jesus. We lift up everyone else except Jesus. When you go to the grocery store, you ought to not be gossiping with everybody. You ought to tell everybody, "Our church is on fire! Our preacher is preaching an uncompromising Gospel." There are many that go around gossiping about the church. But let me tell them today, and tell the devil, "All you're doing is cutting yourself off, because God's justice will prevail."

Jesus said that the devil would come against the church, but the church would prevail, because of the foundation. I'm glad! I can go on today with the Lord! Oh, bless His name today! But I say, if you're guilty, oh, stop it! Oh, stop it! If you're thinking about it, don't do it. I want to say today, you don't have to hang a sign that you've been delivered: just live your life for the Lord. I try, every second of the day, to do the will of God. I'm always praying, "Lord, not my will, but Your will in every situation, Your will in every thought, Your will." Oh, bless His name today! I'm glad today! Sometimes I'm right and sometimes I'm wrong. But I thank the Lord that through it all, I've learned to trust in Jesus. I don't have to brag on Jesus. All I have to do is tell somebody, let my little light shine. Lights can't talk. Lights are not known as great spots of information.

Your light ought to shine. Yes, that's all they do. They shine! I come to tell you this morning, you can shine without showing off. You can pray without showing off. You can shout without showing off. You can preach without showing off. You can testify without showing off. I'm glad this morning! I can't keep it to myself! One Sunday morning – oh, bless the Name of the Lord – the Lord filled me! Oh, He filled me up. I just can't keep it inside! I just can't keep it to myself. He filled me with the precious Holy Ghost. Oh, glory to God. I can go on today, I can tell somebody, "I know the Lord will make a way. I know the Lord can turn my midnights into days."

I just can't keep it to myself this morning. I'm glad that Jesus was hanging there. I'm glad the blood ran down from His hands and His feet. I just can't keep it to myself today. Everywhere I go, I have to tell them, I know the Man from Galilee. I know a Man that can fix you up. I'm glad today. I'm glad for Jesus hanging there, on that cross, blood running down from His hands and His feet. I'm glad today. I'm glad He died on the cross! I just can't keep it to myself! I'm glad this morning! I'm glad Jesus died for us. He shed His blood on Calvary's cross. I'm glad this morning! They placed Him in that borrowed tomb, that cold, dark tomb, all by Himself, — oh, bless His name — but Sunday morning, I see the angels coming down, all the way from heaven, and rolling the stone away. I'm glad this morning, they rolled the stone away, that big, old stone, they rolled it away. They rolled it away! And my Jesus got up with all power. My Jesus! He got up with all power! One day, let me tell you, I'm going to lay down this body!

I did the funeral of a dear sister a couple days ago. She looked like doll lying in that casket. But let me tell you today, her Spirit is with God. Oh, bless His name today!

I'm glad that Jesus rose from the grave with all power in His hands. He got on a cloud and He went all the way back to glory. I'm glad this morning! He sent me Something. He sent the Holy Ghost, down on the inside. You ought to tell somebody; not tell anybody about what somebody else's business is, but you ought to tell somebody, "I know Jesus for myself! He's working in my life." I'm glad this morning! I'm glad this morning! I'm glad I can't keep it to myself! I'm glad this morning, I've got a testimony that the world didn't give and the world can't take away. I'm glad this morning! I'm glad I know the Lord! I know Him for myself.

I want to testify here. I just can't keep it to myself. Everywhere I go, I have to tell somebody. The other day, some people saw me, and they said to me, "You must be a preacher." I said, "Yes, I am. I'm a child of God." And I began to not be able to keep it to myself. Before I knew it, I was telling them about the church. I was telling them about the Spirit of God. I was telling them that nobody can do me like Jesus. I could've gone another way. I could've begun to talk about the baseball game they had on. I could've begun to talk gossip with them. But I told them, "Oh, yes! I'm a preacher, and let me tell you, I know the Lord can make away for you. I know the Lord can turn your midnights into days, I know the Lord can bless you today." Nobody can do me like Jesus. I'm thankful to the Lord this morning. I'm thankful to God, for what He's doing.

As I close this morning, I say to you, don't keep it to yourself. Tell somebody about the Lord. I'm glad this morning! I'm glad today! I can call on the name of the Lord. If you're here this morning, and you need the Lord first in your life, you can come now.

Let me close with this testimony this morning. At the funeral the other day, we gave an invitation to Christ, at the funeral service. As I walked out of the funeral chapel, thanking God for how He had used me during the funeral, there was a young man walking in the parking lot, looking around.

I said to him, "Is something wrong?"

He said, "The ride that I came with, the person had to leave, and I don't have a way home."

I said, "Can you ride with someone else?"

He said, "I don't have anyone else." Then he said, "I need to go now."

I said, "Where are you going?"

He mentioned a street, and I said, "Do you know how to get there?"

He said, "Yes." I said, "Well, I'll drop you off."

He got in the car and we talked. He said to me, "I want to be a Christian."

I said, "You can become a Christian right now."

I had prayer with him when I got over to his house. I found out through talking with him, he was the grandson of the lady I just funeralized. We don't know who we're testifying to. I could have very easily gone in the other direction, but this was the grandson of the woman who had just been funeralized. Because of the Word, it planted a seed. I don't know how far it's going to go. Someone else will come along and reap the harvest, but we are nothing more than the planters of seeds. Jesus, the mighty Lamb of God, is the One who will separate the wheat from the chaff.

We're grateful to God for what He has done, and for what He's going to do.

You can come to Jesus right now.

Don't Forget Who You Are
Job 17:14, Job 25:6, Psalm 8:4-5

We're thankful to the Lord for each of you today. We ask ourselves the question, "Is there a Word from the Lord?" And truly, I want to say to you, there's always a Word from God. It may not come in the way you want to hear it, it may not come in the way you think it should come, but there is always a word from God.

I'm mindful of a story of a boy who was walking down the street with his father at night. They had a lantern, or a light that they would swing. As they were walking along, the father said to the boy, "Son, I want you to wait here until I return. I'll be back, and I want you take the light and just wait until I come. I won't be gone long."

So the boy sat there on a stump, waiting for his father to return. As the boy was waiting there, it began to get dark. Then he began to hear loud noises like animals in the background. People began walking by him. They said to one another, "Why is he sitting there, with that light like that? He should be moving on." Others things came up during the night. The boy was fearful, yet he held the light that his father had given him.

When daybreak was coming, his father came to where he had left the boy. The boy said to his father, "Father, you can't imagine what happened. Last night, there were all kinds of noises. But I still held onto the light. Different ones came by, and they began to laugh at me, as I was sitting on this stump, holding onto this light. After that, other things began to happen, but I still held on to the light. Now you came to get me, and I've still got the light."

I want to say to you this morning, do you have a light? You might say, "What kind of light do I need?" Do you have a light for Jesus? Do you have a light in the midst of the darkness, in the midst of all that's going on around you, even with your own families? Do you have a light that you can hold up for the Lord, and be a testimony for Him? Truly, I can say today, I have a light, and that light is the light of Jesus. Jesus said that if He be lifted up, He would draw all men. We're thankful to God today, that we, too, have a light when we have accepted Jesus Christ as our personal Savior. We, too, have a light when we have asked the Lord to come into our lives, and to live and to move and to take control of situations. That is the light that we are speaking of today.

Would you turn with me in your Bibles this morning, to our text today, to Job, the 25th chapter. We have several scriptures that we will be looking at: Job 25:6 and Job 17:14. In conjunction with that, Psalms 8:4-5. Let us read those verses this morning, beginning with Psalm 8:4.

8:4. What is man, that thou art mindful of him? and the son of man, that thou visitest him?
5. For thou hast made him a little lower than the angels, and hast crowned him with glory and honour.

Then let us turn to Job 17:14:

17:14. I have said to corruption, Thou art my father: to the worm, Thou art my mother, and my sister.

Then Job 25:6 reads to us today:

25:6. How much less man, that is a worm? and the son of man, which is a worm?

Those two books and four verses are what we want to share this morning.

Let us bow our heads in a moment of prayer.

Gracious Father, we come to You today, and Lord God, as we come to You, we come looking to You for strength. We come looking to You, Lord God, that You would lend us Your Spirit. Oh, heavenly Father, we praise You today. We praise You for Your Word, for You said heaven and earth would pass away, but Your Word would stand forever. Truly we thank You, Lord God, for we are the light of the world. And Father, we thank You today, that as we worship in and out of this building, on a daily basis, we are letting the community and the world know that we believe in that light which is Jesus Christ. Oh, heavenly Father, we praise You now, for what You are going to do in the service.

Lord God, use me in a mighty way. Not my will, but let Thy will be done. Oh, heavenly Father, we pray now that the Word of God would go out from beyond these walls, out into the hedges and highways where it would touch men, women, boys and girls. Oh, heavenly Father, we praise You, Lord God, for what You've done, are doing and are going to do, in the mighty name of Jesus. Lord God, we know where we've been, we know where we are, but we don't know where we're going. But Lord God, You hold our future in the palm of Your hands. We praise You for that today. We praise You, Lord God, for You sit high, and You look low. We praise You, Lord God, that we can call upon Your name. We praise You, Lord God, that all good and perfect gifts come from You. Oh, heavenly Father, we thank You right now, that we have a joy that the world didn't give, and the world can't take away. Thank You, Lord God, for this place of worship, and the ones that go in and out of these doors. Thank You, Lord God, in the midst of darkness, that you are our light. Now Lord, strengthen our faith today, in the name of Jesus, as we stand on Your Word. Those, Lord God, who are weak in the faith, You strengthen their faith today, according to Your Word and Your will. Thank You, Lord God, for what you're doing and going to do at Everlasting, in Jesus' name we pray, and we give You the glory right now. Help us, Lord God, to be and to do what it is that You want us to do. Help us, Lord God, to stand on Your Word in this hour. Help us, Lord God, to know who You are. In Jesus' name we pray, and we give You the glory right now, in Jesus' name, amen.

I want to talk about, for a few minutes today, the thought of the subject, "Don't forget who you are." Would you say that with me this morning? Don't forget who you are. As an opening statement today, many of us have forgotten who we are. You might say to me, "Pastor, what do you mean by that? What do you mean, we have forgotten who we are?" If you look around today, you can look at society. You can see from every aspect of society, it dictates this, that and the other. For every situation that's happening today, society has a way of addressing that area. But I'm saying this morning, "Don't forget who you are." Regardless to what society says, regardless to what the ground rules for society are, don't forget who you are. Many of us today, as I said, have forgotten who we are.

I'm mindful this morning that when we did the Martin Luther King Birthday sermon down in front of the City Hall, I mentioned in the message on that day that if Dr. King were here on that day, what would he have to say to us? What would he say if he came back, 20 years later, for a moment, what would be his message to the world? I said, on that particular day, I felt he would say, "Go back to where you were. Go back to when love was genuine. Go back to when people had compassion for one another. Go back to when you really loved your neighbors, not for what you could get out of them, not for what they could get out of you, but you had compassion for them, whether they were up or down." You don't find that much any more. We have situations where neighbors live next door to one another for years and years and they don't even know what their neighbors' names are. We have situations where family members are torn and they don't even speak to one another. They have built up this wall between one another and they care nothing about one another. I was talking to a member of our church and she was saying it had been 30 years since she had spoken to her father. I said to her, "Oh, what a Christian attitude you have, or don't have! In thirty years you have not even tried to get in touch with your father? And you know where he is, and you know his address, and you probably even know his number." Don't forget who you are.

Lots of folks forget who they are. Many in the church have forgotten who they are. Well, you might say, "Pastor, I know who I am. I was born on such and such day, I'm the mother or father of this person or that person. I've done this and done that." But that's not the kind of identity that I'm relating to this morning. Sure, you know who you are, as far as where you were born and those kinds of things. But do you know who you are, with God? Have you forgotten the calling God has on your life?

We knock on doors in this neighborhood every Saturday. We were knocking on doors and giving out tracts yesterday, and I would say that a third of the tracts that we gave out, as we knocked on doors, those folks woke up this morning not knowing who they were. Oh, they knew where they lived and what their address was, and those kinds of things, but spiritually, they were dead. Lots of us have lost our identity as to who we are.

The Bible determines who we are. Our political survival determines who we are. Our society, mostly, determines whether or not we know who we are. The Psalmist, as we read, asks the question, "What is man, that thou art mindful of him? and the son of man, that thou visitest him?"

"What are you saying in that reading, Pastor?" I'm simply saying that each of us, and many of the ones in the world today, take it for granted that they are who they are because of what they are. But I want to say today, that you're just like me. We're nothing more than filthy rags in the sight of God. We all have sinned and come short of the glory of God. But do you know who you are this morning? Don't forget who you are, in Christ Jesus.

Man is a funny creature. If you love him, he will hate you. If you give him truth, he will deceive you. If you lift him up, he will walk on you. This question has plagued every generation, and it goes beyond what scientific definition describes. What I'm saying is that we are who we are only when we are in Christ. Outside of Christ, we are nothing more than filthy rags. Oh, I'm glad today. I'm glad that I have a foundation that is based, not on the world, but a foundation that's based upon Christ Jesus. You might say this morning, where are the masses? Where are the ones who need to know who they are, that were out at the crack house all last night? Where are the ones who need to know who they are, that left the taverns at 2:00 this morning, all drunk out of their minds? Where are the ones this morning who are confused in their own homes today? Do they know who they are? And where are they this morning? I want to say today that the devil is a deceiver.

Even our own church, this place, this building right here, should be full today, of persons knowing who they are. But many don't know that. They think they know who they are. They think they are applying the right things to their lives to get the answers to who they are, but oh, no! They don't know. And who's to blame for this? Is it my fault? Is it your fault? Is it someone's fault in the United States Congress? Is it the President's fault? Oh, no, it's not. It's their own fault. Each one of us will have to stand before the Lord, before God on that great day, and give an account of our deeds and misdeeds. Each one of us will have to stand before the Lord and say, "Lord, it's not them, but it's me." Oh, bless His name today.

I'm mindful this morning that we need to know who we are. And we need not to forget who we are. Sometimes our bodies go further than what man says we are because of where our heart is headed. When I have been deceived, my heart is broken. When those that I love have turned into enemies, there's nothing in the doctor's office, nothing in the drug store that can heal a broken heart. Only that which comes from outer space. You might say, "What's outer space? Are you talking about from the moon, or from the stars, or from some distant planet?" I'm talking about only that which comes from God.

I do marital counseling three months out of the year, January, February and March, and I'll be glad when March is over. I've done so much marital counseling that I'm just burned out already, and I've got a month to go, so you pray for me. I've got one month to go. I set aside just three months for marital counseling, and believe me, it gets heavy. But I say to those ones with a broken heart, nothing in a drug store can heal a broken heart. Nothing that man has, the books, or the technology, or the sociology, or the psychology: nothing can heal a broken heart; only that which comes from Jesus. "As I have been with Moses, so will I be with you. I was with Moses in Israel, and I promise that I will be with you also."

We are pilgrims on this earth. We came from this earth, from dust, and to dust shall we return. Some of us are different in color, but we come from the same Mother Earth. We come from the same place. Somebody said to me the other day, "You're black, and he's white." But I said, it's the same God! God is no respecter of persons. What He has done for them, He will do the same for you. What He is doing for me, He'll do the same for others. Someone said to me the other day, "People don't want to hear that kind of message. They don't want to be challenged to get up off their duffs and get busy for God. And they won't want to hear that." They sure won't. People would rather hear a kind of message that they'll feel good about. They want to hear the kind of message that they can leave from the sanctuary saying, "Oh, didn't he talk nicely about the birds? Oh, weren't the flowers that he described so elegant?" But the flowers and the birds can't save you! Only Jesus can save you! The birds and the flowers can't give you life! Only Jesus can give you life! But how many want to hear that?

We return to earth, and we find everything that we need, like our earthly mother. No one can console us or can deal with us like Mother. I'm a witness to that today. There's something about Mother's touch. No other person can match a mother. I can remember when I was afraid, in the back room one time. Mother would come, and she would spread cover over me. We lived in a house down south that was up off the ground, and it was a peculiar situation, but Mother would come, and she would cover me up. She would touch me, and just one touch made the fear that I had vanish. Nobody can satisfy us like a mother. When I would get hurt, Mother would just look at it and she would kiss it, and she would say, "Junior, it's going to be all right."

Everything that we need, Mother Earth also has it. Oh, I'm glad today. Mother Earth has everything that we need. When we get sick, most of our medicines come from her. Most of our pain pills come from her bosom. They are dressed up and called many new names, but if we trace back, we will find they all come from Mother Earth. Like our earthly mother, she has everything that we need, the love, the tender care, the concern about how we're getting along. She has it all. I remember, when I'd get sick, Mother would come. She had everything in her sack to make me feel strong and young again. My mother lives back East. There's something about it, if she'd call me right now, I don't care what I would be going through, just her voice to me would make everything all right. One thing about my mother, she didn't whip us very much. She had a way of talking to us that made us cry. We'd do something, and she would say, "Come here." She would sit us down, and before we knew it, we would just be crying like a baby, and she hadn't laid a hand on us. That was Mother.

But we're talking today about a different mother. Not only does everyone have an earthly father, we also have an eternal Father, an everlasting Father, a Father who said He would be there in the midst of the storm, a Father who said He would not leave you or forsake you. God came down from glory. He reached into Mother Earth, and He molded man in His hand, and He breathed the breath of life, and man became a living soul. Oh, I'm glad about that. I'm glad I know who I am.

Everybody ought to look a little bit like Mother and a little bit like Father. I may not have my father's hair, or I may not walk like him, but somewhere my father ought to be showing in me. God ought to be showing through every one of us. It ought to be a situation that whatever you're dealing with, God ought to shine through. I don't care how low down a person is, or how mean they are, they have a little bit of God in them.

I know everyone has not only an earthly mother and father, but a heavenly Father, an eternal Father. A little bit of eternity is in them. How do I know this? Because I'm blessed in this darkness to stand on the edge of this world and gaze over into glory land every once in awhile.

"What are you saying, Pastor?" I'm saying that every now and then, I think about going home. I think about going to be with Jesus. I think about the streets that are paved with gold. They're fighting for gold over here, look at the Dow Jones stock market, it's fluctuating every day, but on the other side — oh bless God's name today — there's no suffering there. There's no fighting over gold and other areas there, because God said we would walk the streets of gold. God has blessed us with pretty good houses to live in. He's blessed us with pretty good cars to ride in, with wheels that roll, a few folks to preach to on Sunday. But somehow, I just can't feel at home in this world.

"What are you saying, Pastor?" I don't feel at home right now. Oh, I've got a comfortable place to stay, and I've got food in the refrigerator, and everything seems to be well, but I don't feel at home. But I'm going home one day. Somebody said that we're in the land of the living, getting ready for the land of the dying. I said "Oh, no!" to that. We're in the land of the dying, getting ready for the land of the living. Look at the newspaper, where this guy killed another guy just a few days ago, over there in Portland, shot him in the face and killed him, right on the spot. And so many other devastating things are happening which lets me know that I must first know who I am, and I must know where I'm going. Don't forget who you are today, Church.

Well, lots of folks have forgotten who they are. From the way they act, they have forgotten who they are. You can tell that they have forgotten who they are. Lots of wives have forgotten who they are. The beautiful fashions and the very clothes that make them appealing, and the sweet-smelling perfumes help them to forget who they are. Oh, but I'm glad today. I'm glad that I have on the perfume of Jesus. I'm glad that I have on the make-up of Jesus. I don't have to put on a false face to wake up in the morning and to greet you at the door. When you come to the door, I can raise up, with the joy of knowing that I've laid in Him all night long; and wake up with the rejoicing Spirit of knowing that I don't have to go to the medicine cabinet to start the day, because I know who I am.

Lots of preachers — let me get on them, too — have forgotten who they are. Lots of deacons have forgotten who they are. Lots of chairpersons and members have forgotten who they are. We have many here, at Everlasting, that have forgotten who they are. I said at the banquet that I went to on Friday night that our membership is 242. Just imagine if we had 242 members as a part of this church, active. We could move this county in a mighty way. But many of them have forgotten who they are! Lots of ushers have forgotten who they are. We have five ushers at our church and they have forgotten who they are. I have seen them sit in every kind of group, and act like everything except a Christian. We forget that we are the salt of the earth. We forget that we are the light of the world. We forget that we are like that city that sat on a hillside. I think that everyone ought to remember who they are. Do you remember who you are today?

As I move on this morning, if you remember who you are, it will have something to do with the way you live. I want to tell you today, if you know who you are, you ought to live like it. If you know who you are, you ought to act like it. When Joseph had been elevated from the low lands of poverty and had been given the keys to the barns of plenty and the wife of the king lay herself before him, it was a good thing that Joseph could remember who he was, and what he was. If you can remember who you are, it will have everything to do with the way you act.

Oh, I'm glad today, God can use me. I'm glad today that I can let this little light shine. We don't sing that much any more, "This little light of mine, I'm gonna let it shine. Everywhere I go, I'm gonna let it shine. Hide it under a bushel? NO! I'm gonna let it shine."

I read in the Bible about some boys on the Babylonian plain. They were a long way from home, way down in Babylon. I've heard those boys, when everyone was bowing down to the graven image, those boys said, "We know who we are." They said to the king, "We will not bow down to the golden image. We will not bow down." They never forgot who they were. If you remember who you are, I declare, it will have something to do with the way you live.

Job said, "Who are we?" We need to know who we are. If I have to be a worm, let me be like this little worm, and let me close with this story today. There's a worm, and this worm really is, in essence, a butterfly. This worm is called a caterpillar. He doesn't always stay in the form of a worm. God has fixed it so he does not have to grow like this all of his life. He does not have a beautiful voice to sing in the choir. He is not known for his great preaching. He doesn't hold an office in the church. But God fixed it so that he can be something else. God will change him from what he is. He clamps up on the bark of a tree. He has to lock his body to the side of that tree. While he is there, he lets out some fluid that fastens to that tree. When it gets hard, he holds fast. After a while, the rain will wash the little body. After a while, the sun will shine on that body and that old body, that old, ugly thing that we look at, on the outside, it turns into a cocoon. Then, he will look like he is dead there, but on the inside, he becomes a new creature. They tell me that he will lay there for a while, and the old body will break open. And when it breaks open, he comes out a beautiful butterfly.

We ought to know who we are. You ought to know that God is in control, not only of this world, but He's in control of your life.

You ought to know that all you've got to do is call upon Him, and He will hear and answer your prayer. Oh, I'm glad today. I'm glad that Jesus, the mighty Lamb of God, knows who you are.

Somebody would say this morning, "Does God know what I'm going through?" Oh, yes, He does. He's got it already written in the book, what will happen in your life. Somebody would say this morning, "Did God know what was going to happen to Jesus in His life?" And I would say, "Oh, yes He did," that God pre-destined it so, that God so loved the world that He sent His only begotten Son. Oh, I'm glad this morning, that Jesus, the mighty Lamb of God, is in control of this world. I'm glad for the mighty Lamb of God.

I want to challenge you today. You ought to know who you are. Let nobody tell you that the Lord is not in control. Let nobody tell you that God doesn't know what's going on. God knows what's happening at this hour. We can stand on the Word of God. We can lean upon His everlasting arms. Let me tell you what Jesus did, when He died on the cross. Jesus loves us so much that He gave His own life that we would have life more abundantly. Many people don't want to know that they are sinners, but I want to let you know today, we all are sinners, and we're only saved by the grace of God. Jesus is still saving. Jesus is still sanctifying. Jesus is still filling with the precious power of the Holy Ghost and fire. I'm glad today. I'm glad today! I can call on His name. I'm glad today, I can stand on His Word.

I tell my family all the time, "Don't look to me, but look to Jesus." He's the only One. He's the only One who can make a way for you. He's the only One who can give you joy where there is no joy. The Spirit of God, the Holy Ghost, is real. If you know who you are, you ought to be able to tell somebody, "I know the Lord. He has been good to me." You ought to have a testimony everywhere you go. I know the Lord is a way-maker. Oh, bless His name today. Let me tell you today, I'm glad, I'm glad today!

I know who I am. Everywhere I go, I can let my light shine. It makes no difference what the world says. I say, "Hold on! Hold on! Hold on to the Lord!" He'll make a way for you! Put your hand, Church, in God's hand. I'm glad, I'm glad! I'm glad this morning, I can lean and depend on His Word.

Are you glad today? Many people don't want to hear this. You ought to have something that the world didn't give and the world can't take away. When the devil comes against you, you ought to have something that you can stand on. Oh, bless God's name. Jesus said to Peter, "Upon this rock, I build my church, and the gates of hell cannot prevail against it." I'm glad! Oh, glory to God! I can lean on His Word. Don't be surprised what's going on all around you, because Jesus said these things would have to come. The Word of God has to be fulfilled. Men are going to talk about peace, but there won't be any peace. Men will talk about joy, but there won't be any joy. Let me tell you today, there's only one true joy! You've got to first know who you are. You can lean on Him, regardless to what you're going through.

Thank You, Lord, for what You're doing. Thank You, Lord, for what You're going to do.

I'm glad. I'm glad today! Oh, bless His name. I'm glad today. Many will call me; you can't imagine how full that recorder is going to be before 7:00 tonight, and many will be asking, "What can you do for me?" I can tell them, "I can't do anything for you. I can pray for you. I can call on the Lord, but you've got to first know who you are." I'm glad about that! I can tell the world, it's not you, but it's Jesus, the Christ that lives within you, that ought to be doing the work.

As I move on here today, look at Jesus, hanging on that cross, blood running down, oh glory to God. You might say this morning, "I wasn't there. I didn't crucify Him. I didn't pierce Him in His side." No, you weren't there, but we do it in a different way. We do it when we lie about one another. We do it when we cheat on one another. We do it when we don't do what the Word says to do. I yield my will to His Spirit and I say, "Lord, not my will, but Thy will be done." Can you say this morning, in whatever area it's in, "It's not my will, Lord?" Oh, glory! I don't know what tomorrow's going to bring, but I know today who I am. I'm washed in the blood of the Lamb. His blood! There's still power in His blood.

You might say, "Do you preach like that everywhere you go?" Everywhere I go, I tell the story, the story of Jesus, the mighty Lamb of God. They hanged Jesus on the cross, for my sins, and your sins, and the sins of the world. He didn't say a mumbling word. All He said was, "Father, forgive them, for they know not what they do." Can you tell somebody, "I forgive you?" Can you tell somebody, "I love you anyhow?" Just say, "Father, You know what's happening here. Father, have Your way!" I believe things will begin to happen in a mighty way.

They put a crown of thorns on His head, but He didn't say a mumbling word. They beat Him, but He didn't say a mumbling word. They took His clothes off His back, but He didn't say a mumbling word. They nailed His hands. They nailed His feet. He didn't say a mumbling word. He died on the cross for the sins of the world. One of the Sunday School kids asked me, "Why did He have to die on the cross?" I said, "For my sins, for your sins, and for the sins of the world." He had to die! Nobody was worthy. If you call Abraham, he wasn't worthy. If you call Moses, he wasn't worthy. If you call Jacob, he wasn't worthy. Nobody was worthy but the Lamb of God. And the Word says that they crucified Him on the cross and they placed Him in a borrowed tomb. All day Saturday, all night Saturday night, He lay there in that tomb. But the Word says, Sunday morning the Spirit of God moved upon Him.

The Spirit of God can move upon you this morning! The Spirit of God can move upon you this morning! The Spirit of God can move upon you this morning! The Spirit of God can move upon you this morning!

It can move upon you this morning, but you have to let It have Its way. The Word of God says, the Spirit of God moves us. It moved upon Jesus, as He lay there. As He lay there, in that cold tomb, the Word says, He got up on Sunday morning. All power was in His hands. He got up with Holy Ghost power. He got up with resurrection power. He got up with all power in His hands. I'm glad today! The same Spirit that got Him up is the same Spirit that's here today. You can have It today! I can't give It to you. Only Jesus can give It to you.

The Word says He got on a cloud, and He went all the way back to glory. He went all the way back, all the way back to His Father, to prepare a place for us. Jesus said, "In my Father's house there are many mansions, and if it were not so, I would have told you." Jesus said, "I'm going back to prepare a place for you."

Let me tell you this morning, you ought to be thankful that this is not your home. I'm going home one day, to be with the Lord! I'm going to see my father there! I'm going to see my sister there! I'm going to see my great grandmother there! Oh, Lord, thank You today. The Spirit of joy! Oh, bless His name. Oh, glory, glory to God. He sent the Spirit.

If you don't know who you are, you can come now. Come to Jesus, just as you are.

An Important Decision
John 7:37-43

We're thankful to Lord this morning for each of you. I want to ask you to turn in your Bibles with me. The question is asked, "Is there a Word from the Lord?" I want to say today that there is always a Word from the Lord. There's always a Word from God. And we're grateful to God that that Word can come in so many different ways and at so many different times.

The man who lost his family, who I mentioned earlier, the question he asked me was, "Why? Why would God take my wife and my two kids in an automobile accident?" He wanted to blame God for that. And I said to Him, "God has a reason for everything. It may not be the reason you can accept, but God has a reason, and I don't know what the reason is." I said to him, "Suppose it was the other way around. Suppose your wife was here with two small kids, mourning your death. How do you think she would feel at this hour?" And I said to him, "Raise your head up. Raise your head up and see beyond what physically is happening right now. See the beauty of God in your situation."

That's what I want to talk about this morning. I want to talk about a subject along those lines. If you would, turn with me to St. John, the 7th chapter, beginning at the 37th verse. I want to say again that we're grateful to the Lord for each of you this morning. We're grateful to God for what He has done, and what He's going to do today. Let's begin at the 37th verse.

37. In the last day, that great day of the feast, Jesus stood and cried, saying, If any man thirst, let him come unto me, and drink.
38. He that believeth on me, as the scripture hath said, out of his belly shall flow rivers of living water.
39. (But this spake he of the Spirit, which they that believe on him should receive: for the Holy Ghost was not yet given; because that Jesus was not yet glorified.)
40. Many of the people therefore, when they heard this saying, said, Of a truth this is the Prophet.
41. Others said, This is the Christ. But some said, Shall Christ come out of Galilee?

42. Hath not the scripture said, That Christ cometh of the seed of David, and out of the town of Bethlehem, where David was?
43. So there was a division among the people because of him.

Do you know there are many church gatherings today where they don't even open their Bibles anymore? There are many church gatherings today where you never hear them preach about hell. You never hear them tell people, "If you're not walking the straight and narrow, you must be on the road to destruction, and the road to destruction is a broad way." You don't hear that much in these times, in this day. But I want to tell you, God is going to hold us responsible. He's going to hold us accountable for what we do or don't do for Him.

Let us pray at this time.

Our Father and our God, we thank You that we can come to You today. Oh, heavenly Father, I just want to get out of the way. I don't want my will to be done, but we're asking that Your will, which is perfect, be done. Oh, Lord God, I pray now that You would use these lips of clay. Oh, heavenly Father, I pray that You would use my mouth, and that You would give me what it is that You would have me to say. Oh, heavenly Father, we pray now that You would open up the ones that are sitting today; open up their eyes, open up their ears, they might not just be hearers, but doers of Your Word. Now, oh, heavenly Father, we thank You for the Spirit that's in this place right now. Oh, heavenly Father, let it manifest within us in a mighty way. Oh, heavenly Father, we thank You, right now. Thank You, Lord, for your Word, for It will not ever pass away. But Your Word will stand forever, and we thank You for it right now. Now, Lord, we pray that You will move in a mighty way, in Jesus' name, the name above every name. In Jesus' name we pray, thank God, thank God, thank God.

I want to talk about this morning from those few verses, the thought of the subject today, "An Important Decision." Many of us are making decisions about a lot of things. I don't know about you, but it seems like every day or every second of my life I'm making some kind of decision. Sometimes it's the wrong decision and sometimes it's the right decision. But we want to talk this morning about an important decision.

You might say, "Pastor, what kind of decision are you talking about? I made a decision about my marriage, and I made a decision about my job. I made a decision about my family. I made a decision about where I'm going to stay." But we're talking today about a very important decision.

Here in these readings we have, number one, a great feast; number two, we have a great day, the last day of the feast; and number three, we have a great preacher, the Christ, the Son of God. We can see in verse 38, in your Bibles which are red letter edition, it's in red. Jesus is saying, "He that believeth on me, as the Scriptures have said, out of his belly shall flow of rivers of living water."

You ought to be rejoicing about that this morning. All you have to do, first of all, is believe on Him, as the scriptures have said, and then, out of your belly shall flow rivers of living water.

I'm concerned today. I'm concerned about Christians as a whole. "What are you saying, Pastor?" I'm saying that as Christians, many of us are standing on something else. Many of us are standing on traditions. Many of us are standing on what mother and father and others have said and done. But the question is in the singular today. "You that believe it, whatever your name may be, you that believe on Me, as the Scriptures have said, out of your belly shall flow rivers of living water."

Here we see this morning, not only do we have a great Preacher, but we have a great Servant. He said, "I am the living water for a thirsty world." I tell you this morning, if you're thirsty today, not for the physical water, if you're thirsty this morning for the living water, you can receive that living water this morning.

Somebody may be saying, "You're talking about the baptism in the Columbia River, Thursday, a week ago." Oh, no, for that river one day will run dry, but out of your belly shall flow rivers of living water that will never run dry. We're talking, this morning, about an important decision. The only way that can happen in your life is that you must make this important decision. Either you're going to spend eternity in heaven with God, or you're going to spend it in hell with the devil.

We also have in this text a great division. For the Word says that there was a division among the people. They were divided, because some said, "What good thing could come out of Nazareth? Nothing good comes out Nazareth." But don't you know, the devil has all kinds of ways of deceiving you and me? He's deceiving millions today, all over this country and all over the world.

Our president was on TV just a few days ago, saying he doesn't eat asparagus. As much as he ought to be doing about our country, they're talking about some garbage. They're talking about something that doesn't mean a thing. They ought to be having a prayer meeting in the White House, reading the Scriptures, asking God to have rivers of living water flowing out of the president's mouth so he might be able to direct this country and our people.

Oh, but look at the devil. Many are being deceived on every hand, but look at the features of this division. Jesus was the Subject of their division. They weren't divided because of some of their gossip. There were divided because of Jesus, the Christ. They were divided about His miracles, because if it hadn't been the miracles that stood forth, they wouldn't have to make a decision. All they had to do was to ask the woman who had the issue of blood, "Who is He that cured you?" She would have said, "He is Jesus, the Christ, for I spent all my money. I had seen every doctor I could see, and I wasn't better. But when I touched the hem of His garment, I was made whole."

Oh, come on up here, the man who had the withered hand. He had a testimony, but it wasn't about those ones that had been touched by the Master, it was among those of the world. Well, let me tell you today, there had to be an important decision. Because of Him, the question was, who was He, and what was He? Was He a good Man? Was He a true prophet, or an imposter?

I want to tell you today, He's my King of kings. He's my Lord of lords. I don't know what the people said then, but I need to ask you also, whom do you say that He is? Is He the Lord of your life? Is He the One, that when your problems get heavy, you can go down on your knees and talk to the Lord? Is He the One, that when they slap you on the one side of your cheek, you can turn the other? I want to tell you today, for they asked the question, "Is He a true prophet or is He an imposter?" And they were divided in their opinions. Let me tell you, some thought He was a prophet. Some said they thought He was the Christ, while others doubted and objected and opposed. Many are doing that today. Many are objecting to who Jesus is. Oh, many want to see signs. "Let me see some sign of who God is." Let me tell you today, He's still working miracles. He's still giving sight to the blind. He's still saving. He's still filling. He's still sanctifying. He's still doing the work that He did then; He's still doing the work today.

It was all-important that they should agree to accept Him, to obey Him. They were divided, while they ought to have been unanimous. They should have been together in agreement, saying, "I know the Man. I was blind one day, and He opened my eyes. I know the Man." But the question today: where were those who were healed, who weren't part of this decision?

I'm mindful this morning of last Sunday's Sunday school lesson, when Jesus was taken to Pilate, the governor. They shoved Him in, and they stood outside, waiting, knowing what the verdict was going to be. Why didn't they call somebody who had been touched by the Master? Why didn't they call someone who had made that important decision? Why didn't they call someone who been healed by the Master's touch? Jesus had told them who He was, in His person, character, and ministry, and in His mighty works, which were in perfect harmony with His claims, in perfect unity and divine fortitude. They pointed to Him as the Son of God. He's still working miracles today.

You might say this morning, you're looking for miracle. I want to tell you today, you can see a miracle right here. God is still working miracles. You don't have to look anywhere else for a miracle. Just look around you. Today we sang that song, "Amazing Grace, how sweet the sound that saved a wretch like me." We all were wretches. We all were undone, but God saved us and brought us out. Division, error, deceits from truth; some said, "He is the Christ," but others doubted and objected. But let me tell you this morning, truth is in order. Truth is in order, because Jesus is still working miracles. He's still giving sight to the blind. He's still opening up blind eyes. When you start talking about Jesus, something begins to happen on inside. It seems like the world is dark in this hour. But Jesus is still the Light of the world. He's still giving sight to the blind.

Someone said to me the other day, "What are you talking about? I don't see the miracles that Jesus is doing." And I said to him, "All you've got to do is open your eyes and open your mind, and let Him come in, and everything will be all right."

Let me tell you this morning, if you haven't made that important decision, you can make it right now.

Some were very displeased with Him. Some didn't like what the Lord had done. But He is the Christ, the Son of the living God.

He is the Lord, not only the Lord of heaven, but He is the Lord of this world. If you haven't made that important decision, you need to make it right now.

I feel, this morning, that the Lord is leading me in another direction. You ought to be careful about the Spirit of God. I don't know why today, but the Spirit has said, "Shut up the Book." Oh, glory to God. Let me tell you this morning, I'm glad! I worked all week on the message, but the Lord has said, "Shut up the Book. I've got something I'm going to feed you all the way from heaven above."

I'm glad today. Maybe you might be going through something. Let me tell you about Shadrach and Meshach and Abednego, what they were going through. When they were placed in that fiery furnace, God didn't deliver them like the king thought, but God delivered them when He got ready, in His own time and in His own way.

Maybe you're going through something, but God will take care of you. He may not deliver you when you want to be delivered, but He'll change your attitude. I'm glad! I'm glad today! God can fix whatever it might be. You can call on Him at the midnight hour. I closed up the Book.

Now feed me, Lord. Feed me, Jesus.

I don't know about you today, but I'm not the keeper of myself. Oh, glory to God! Thank You, Jesus! I'm glad this morning! We can stand on His Word! Oh, bless His name today!

Let me say today, I better move on. Oh, bless God. Let me tell you this morning, you don't know like I know what the Lord has done for me. I tell you today, you can stand on His Word. As I move on here, I'm glad today. I made a decision to follow the Lord; not just on Sunday, not just on Monday, but every day, working and talking with the Lord. He'll make everything, everything! — He'll make everything all right. Oh, bless His name today!

As I move on here today, I'm glad. I'm glad for Jesus, the mighty Lamb of God. Let me tell you today, nobody, nobody, nobody can do you like the Lord. Stand on His Word. Nobody can dress you up. Nobody can fix you up. Nobody, this morning, can give you joy on the inside, and peace that passes all understanding. I'm glad this morning. If you haven't made that Important Decision, you can make it right now. Oh, bless His name today. You can stand on His Word!

But look at Jesus hanging on that cross, blood running down from His hands and His feet, but He didn't say a mumbling word, but "Father, My Father, forgive them, for they know not what they do."

If you're here this morning, and you can't say "Father," — not your earthly father, but the Father above, the One that can change midnight into day, the One that can bring you out — you can call on Him right now. I'm glad this morning! I can call on the name of Christ. You ought to have Jesus on the inside. You ought to have Jesus. Oh, glory to God, rivers of living water flowing out of your bellies. I'm glad!

As I move on here, I'm glad I made a decision of Who I'm going to follow. I'm going to follow Jesus, all the way, all the way! You can, today, make the decision to follow Lord, not just on Sundays, not just on Mondays, but every day of the week! Let me move on this morning. I'm glad today! I'm glad for the move of God, that He is real! He's real! He's real!

My grandmother would say, "Who wouldn't serve a good God like this?" Let me tell you, He is good. I know He is good. All you've got to do is make a decision. Make a decision.

All you need to do is have a sincere heart, and say, "Jesus, I need you, Jesus. I love you, Jesus. I want you, Jesus." If you haven't made that decision to follow the Lord already, you can make that decision right now.

Thank You, Lord, that You died there on that cross, blood running down from Your hands and Your feet. They pierced You in Your side.

He did it for me and He did it for you. I don't have to die. I can live in the Lord. Many are dying on every hand. But I'm going to live with Jesus. I'm going to reign with my King. Don't you worry, if you never see me again, if you read in the newspaper that I was killed, or I died. I'm going up a little bit higher.

You might say, "Why are you talking like that?" But I've got a home on the other side. Oh, bless His name. No more suffering there. No more lying there. No more backbiting, no more cheating, no more sorrow there. I've got a home on the other side. Thank You, Lord. Oh, thank You, Lord. I'm going to see my Jesus.

You can choose Jesus right now. You can make that important decision. Jesus is calling you. Come to Jesus.

About the Author

Pastor Willie F. Pride, Jr. is the founder of Everlasting Missionary Baptist Church in Vancouver, Washington, where he was the senior pastor for 30 years. The Lord has blessed him to baptize hundreds of people, many in the Columbia River. He has dedicated many babies to the Lord and he has performed hundreds of weddings and homegoing services. He has been involved with a TV ministry that has been shown in Vancouver for nearly 20 years, as well as in Portland, Oregon, and five other cities in Washington State. He has been active in neighborhood evangelism, prison ministry, hospital ministry, and nursing home ministry. Everywhere he goes, Pastor Pride takes the opportunity to share the goodness of God with everyone he meets.

Pastor Pride is married to Dana Pride, and they have one son living at home, one daughter in college, three grown sons, three grown daughters, 24 grandchildren and 5 great-grandchildren.

Additional copies of this book can be ordered by sending your name and address with a check or money order for $7.95 + $3.95 shipping & handling (total = $11.90) made payable to:

Everlasting Publishing
P.O. Box 1061
Yakima, WA 98907-1061
USA

http://everlastingpublishing.org

Coming soon!
The Meat of the Word for Christians Today, Volume 2
"Everyone Needs Jesus"